Fifty Two Days of Grace

Fifty Two Days of Grace

A devotional based on Paul's
letter to the Romans

Cindy Boose

Fifty Two Days of Grace
Copyright © 2014 Cindy Boose

Unless otherwise noted, all scriptures are taken from THE HOLY BIBLE, NEW INTERNATIONAL VERSION®, NIV® Copyright © 1973, 1978, 1984, 2011 by Biblica, Inc.® Used by permission. All rights reserved worldwide.

Photography and makeup by Vanessa Boose

Cover design by Paul Strand

ISBN-13: 978-1495912511
ISBN-10: 1495912515

Printed in the United States of America

This book is dedicated to Jesus Christ,
without whose sacrifice I would never
know of the amazing grace
on which I now stand.
(Romans 5:1-2)

I would like to thank my family whose support has meant the world to me, especially to my dear husband who believes in me even when I don't, and to my four beautiful daughters whose godly wisdom and advice defy their years. To my mother, my biggest fan, for your ready words of encouragement and to my dad whose humor and love for people runs through my veins. Thank you to both of you for your love and support throughout the years.

To my older sister Susan who inspires me to see the world through the eyes of a child and my little sister Debby whose example has taught me more about living as a godly wife and mother than any number of sermons ever could.

My heartfelt gratitude goes to the women of Bayview Writers who sparked my passion for the written word but especially to Liza Montes who graciously invited me into their special company. I also want to recognize my friend and fellow writer May Vokaty who gave me the encouragement and wisdom I needed to carry this project through the finish line and to Marilyn Buckmaster whose love and grace spurs me on. I could not have finished this project without the support and expert assistance of Paul Strand who designed my cover and formatted the manuscript. I also thank my dear friend Diane Steele; her eager willingness to lend a helping hand made completing this project a joy.

Mostly, though, I would like to thank Jesus Christ my Lord and Savior whose sacrifice on the cross made it possible for me to taste and see that the Lord is good. Words can hardly express what I feel in my heart for a God who would take a broken, insecure, fearful and doubting shell of a woman and fill her with such an indescribable power that she is able to do more than she could ever ask or imagine. My heart is forever grateful. I love you, Jesus!

Know Thyself in Christ

"Paul, a servant of Christ Jesus, called to be an apostle and set apart for the gospel of God." (Romans 1:1)

Paul did not have an identity problem. He knew his position in the scheme of things, and he knew who he followed. He also knew his calling in life. With this information firmly ingrained in his being, he was able to unquestionably and unwaveringly forge ahead on his mission.

For those of us whose position and calling may not be so clear, life can be a constant struggle. To whom do we listen? Which way do we go? Who do we follow? What activities do we do and which do we discard? What is a part of our mission, and what is not?

Henry David Thoreau knew the importance of knowing one's purpose. He said, "Many men go fishing all of their lives without knowing that it is not fish they are after." Knowing why God placed us on this earth at this moment saves years of wasted time. Even Plato understood this concept on some level as evidenced by his philosophy that, "The life which is unexamined is not worth living."

Knowing who we are makes clear
where we go and what we do.

Fifty Two Days of Grace

How can knowing your position as a servant of Christ Jesus, instead of as an independent, maker-of-your-own-destiny kind of person, change your perspective on life?

Read Jeremiah 29:11-13. Have you purposefully sought out the purpose God has for your life?

What fears, doubts or plans of your own are getting in the way of God's plan for your life?

Heavenly Father,
*   I know you have made me for a purpose. Everything You do is with Your sovereign plan in mind. Help me to trust You with that plan, despite my own weaknesses. May Your name be glorified in my life as I learn to walk by faith.*
In Jesus' name I pray,
Amen.

Promises Kept

"Paul, a servant of Christ Jesus, called to be an apostle and set apart for the gospel of God— the gospel he promised beforehand through his prophets in the Holy Scriptures." (Romans 1:1-2)

"But Mom, you promised!" I don't know how many times I've heard that desperate cry from the mouths of disappointed children. As parents, it's common to break a promise. We may have every intention of keeping our pledge, but, life happens, circumstances change, and our ability to fulfill that guarantee falls through.

God, however, does not have that problem!

The promise of our salvation through Jesus Christ was given all the way back in Abraham's time when God said, "All nations will be blessed through you." (Genesis 12:2-3 and Galatians 3:8) What a God of planning and forethought we worship!

Since we know the One True God is a God who keeps promises, we can trust Him with our very lives. If He can fulfill prophecies made thousands of years before the birth of the Messiah, can He not free us from the bondage of worry, or the desire to control, or the pit of despair? Yes, He can. He has more than shown His trustworthiness. Now it's time to show our *trust in Him* by *surrendering all to Him.*

Fifty Two Days of Grace

"Faith is two empty hands held open to receive all of the Lord Jesus." --Alan Redpath

How do you place God in the same category as man, assuming He will let you down?

What area of your life do you struggle with surrendering to the One who loves you unconditionally?

Have you sometimes said, "It's not God I don't trust, it's me! I'm the one who will mess it all up." How is this attitude showing a lack of respect for the Sovereignty and Power of God?

Heavenly Father,

Thank You for being the One who I can trust completely. You will never let me down. Help me to forget all the bad experiences I've had with people and judge You completely based on Your own merits as a loving, Promise-Keeper. When I am tempted to use my own frailties as an excuse for not trusting You, remind me of Moses who also let his pride get in the way of following You without reserve. You are a God who is in control and I place my life in Your hands.

In Jesus' Name I pray,

Amen.

Called

"And you also are among those Gentiles who are called to belong to Jesus Christ. To all in Rome who are loved by God and called to be his holy people: Grace and peace to you from God our Father and from the Lord Jesus Christ." (Romans 1:6-7)

Just think; the Creator of all things is calling us to belong to Him through faith in Jesus Christ! God is at once all-powerful, yet personal enough to know us intimately. As lost as the Romans were, and we now are as self-absorbed, pleasure-seeking beings; God is calling us. He is calling us right now to surrender to Him. He is calling us to stop living for ourselves, and to live for His glory. "You are not your own; you were bought at a price. Therefore honor God with your body." (I Corinthians 6:20)

But how? Verse 7 of today's reading gives us the answer: through the grace given to us from Father and Son. Charles Spurgeon knew that we cannot accomplish anything in our own power, apart from the grace of God when he said, "All that is good or ever will be good in us is preceded by the grace of God and is the effect of a Divine cause within." It is this very grace, in fact, that gives us another moment of life and breath with which to utter a prayer of surrender, *I give my life to You this moment, for You to do as You please in order to bring glory to Yourself.*

Fifty Two Days of Grace

God sent Jesus to us, God calls us,
God gives us grace to accept.

Grace can be defined as getting what you don't deserve.
This world talks a lot about what you deserve. You
deserve to be treated well, you deserve a break, etc. How
does this line of thought run counter to the teaching of
Romans 1:6 and I Corinthians 6:20?

What gets in the way of God having His way in your
life?

Read I Samuel 15 where Samuel confronts King Saul's
disobedience to God's instructions. How did Saul show
disregard for the specific instructions God gave him
through the prophet Samuel? How do you show
disregard for the specific instructions God gave you
through His written word?

Heavenly Father,
*   I admit I do not take your calling seriously. You*
have given me everything I need in order to accomplish
what you have called me to do, but I fail to fully
surrender my all to You. Thank You for the grace with
which You have flooded me, and help me to appreciate
how much I depend on that grace for every breath,
despite my own lack of merit. Help me to accept the
grace You have given to me so that You can fully have
Your way in my life.
In Jesus' Name I pray, Amen

Wield Your Weapons

"First, I thank my God through Jesus Christ for all of you, because your faith is being reported all over the world. God, whom I serve in my spirit in preaching the gospel of his Son, is my witness how constantly I remember you in my prayers at all times; and I pray that now at last by God's will the way may be opened for me to come to you." (Romans 1:8-10)

There are many people we can thank God for putting in this world: Believers who inspire others by their great faith, those who teach many by using their gifts, or some who take a bold stand for Christ in the face of persecution. It is important that we remember to pray for these saints as often as they come to mind.

We, as followers of the Christ, are on the front lines of a spiritual battle and prayer is one of our offensive weapons. After describing our defensive armor in this battle, Paul goes on in Ephesians 6:10-18 to give us our weapons. The word of God is one and prayer is the other. "And pray in the Spirit on all occasions with all kinds of prayers and requests. With this in mind, be alert and always keep on praying for all the saints." (Ephesians 6:18)

Just as a soldier in combat is wise to not let his guard down, nor be without his firearm, we should always stay alert and constantly use the weapon of prayer.

Martin Luther knew a little something about spiritual warfare in his quest to break from the Catholic Church in the 16th Century. He said, "Prayer is a strong wall and a fortress of the church; it is a goodly Christian weapon."

Wield your weapons, followers of
Jesus: Pray without ceasing.

Do you take prayer as seriously as you should?

List some brothers and sisters in Christ for whom you could commit to praying on a regular basis.

How can you help yourself to remember to wield your offensive weapons more often, as if in the midst of battle?

Heavenly Father,

I know there is a battle raging in the heavenly realms even though I cannot see it. Help me to remember to keep Your people in my prayers in order to do my part in this battle. Help me also to keep in mind that the One who is in me is greater than the One who is in the world. Thank You for being my rock, my fortress and my salvation. In You I will ever praise!
I pray these things in Jesus' Name,
Amen

True Hope

"I remember you in my prayers at all times; and I pray that now at last by God's will the way may be opened for me to come to you. I long to see you so that I may impart to you some spiritual gift to make you strong— that is, that you and I may be mutually encouraged by each other's faith. I do not want you to be unaware, brothers and sisters, that I planned many times to come to you (but have been prevented from doing so until now) in order that I might have a harvest among you, just as I have had among the other Gentiles." (Romans 1:10-13)

I wonder whatever happened to Sally? She was a good friend, but after she moved, I never heard from her again.

There are people who were important in our past with which we've lost contact; it happens to everyone. It's easy to think they don't care or that they don't value our friendship, but maybe that is not the case.

Our lives tend to go in cycles, and God puts some people there for a season. But experiencing physical estrangement doesn't necessarily mean their heart is not with us, nor ours with them.

Paul longed to visit the believers in Rome, but God had kept him busy preaching to those who hadn't heard the Gospel. It was important to Paul that they knew he was constantly praying for them. It's the same with us. Even though God may keep us occupied in a job that keeps us from those we miss, we can still join them in spirit through prayer.

Following Jesus may mean we will be apart from those with whom we long to see, but we can have the hope of an eternity together with those who follow Christ. This hope makes conditions here on earth bearable.

True hope seeks only the Kingdom of God.

How are you putting your own desires to be near friends or family above God's calling on your life?

Are there people with whom you've lost contact against whom you are holding a grudge? Could you start praying for them instead?

How does keeping your eyes on the rewards waiting in heaven help you to endure the temporary separation here on earth?

Heavenly Father,

I admit I have sometimes put my own feelings ahead of Your calling for my life. I want nothing more than to go where You send me, but I am afraid to let go of the people in my life. I ask you for the strength to trust You in all things, and to remember to pray for those I miss.
I pray these things in Jesus' name,
Amen

Irresistible Power

"For I am not ashamed of the gospel, because it is the power of God that brings salvation to everyone who believes: first to the Jew, then to the Gentile. For in the gospel the righteousness of God is revealed—a righteousness that is by faith from first to last, just as it is written: 'The righteous will live by faith.'" (Romans 1:16-17)

I remember hearing a story about a man who refused to accept the gospel for his entire life until the age of 80, at which time he tearfully and humbly acknowledged his need for Christ as his Savior. What could possibly have softened his heart?

Clearly, there was a force at work in this man's life that was beyond his own control. Similarly, I remember my own salvation experience around the age of 10 at a Billy Graham Crusade where I was irresistibly drawn forward. It wasn't anything of my own doing or of anyone's influence. Instead, it was an undeniable pulling of the power of God found in the message of salvation through Jesus Christ that compelled me forward. I couldn't help but accept this message. It was my time.

The very faith that we use to put our lives in God's hand is a gift from God by His grace. If it were by our own wherewithal that we believed, then it would be by our own power that we would save ourselves. But God is clear in telling us we are not saved by works, "For it is by grace you have been saved, through faith-and this is not from yourselves, it is a gift of God-not by works so that no-one can boast." (Ephesians 2:8)

Maybe Martin Luther said it best: "God has taken my salvation out of the control of my own will, and put it under the control of His, and promised to save me."

We can rest easy knowing that each one's salvation is in God's hands.

How can this knowledge give you peace about a loved one who has not accepted Jesus as his Savior?

Do you ever think that there is something you must do in order to earn salvation, thinking that it can't be as easy as trusting in Jesus or that you must have to at least try to be good? How can this line of thinking lead to pride and a judgmental attitude?

Is God drawing you, or has He already, toward trusting in Jesus as your Savior? Explain

Heavenly Father,

I thank You for Your gift of grace which gives me the faith to trust in Jesus as my Savior. Thank You for this amazing gift of salvation, and help me to always fight against the temptation to try to be good enough for Heaven. Help me to remember Your patience, grace and love for me and to extend that to others.

In Jesus' Name I pray,
Amen

Fifty Two Days of Grace

Finger Pointing

"For in the gospel the righteousness of God is revealed—a righteousness that is by faith from first to last, just as it is written: 'The righteous will live by faith.'" (Romans 1:17)

"Those so-called Christians…"

"So-and-So says she's a Christian, but she sure doesn't act like one."

Maybe you've heard a brother or sister in Christ utter these words, or maybe you've said them yourself. It's easy to take the law, and apply it to everyone else and point out where they fall short.

William Faulkner said, "All of us failed to match our dreams of perfection." Others' shortfalls seem to glare out at us, but not one of us is capable of doing everything right. We all fall short: Thus, our need for a Savior. (Romans 3:23)

Under the new covenant, we are made right before the Lord by faith. "This is accomplished from start to finish by faith." (Romans 1:17 NLT)

There is not one bit of evidence that through our own effort anyone can look more Christ-like. It is only our faulty human perspective that expects so much of others.

Acknowledging our need for Jesus in every waking moment leads to a humility that won't allow finger-pointing. None of us looks like a Christian apart from faith in Jesus. This is a moment-by-moment act of surrendering. Our fingers, unfortunately, are drawn to point out the flesh in all of us.

Focus on Christ found in each of us, not on the flesh struggling for attention.

In what areas of your life do you most struggle with seeing other believers' sin?

How much time do you spend applying God's Word to your own areas of sin in comparison to how much you direct it toward others?

How much do you focus on Jesus throughout the day? What if you replaced those thoughts of others with thoughts of Jesus and what He has done for you?

Heavenly Father,
It is so easy for me to point the finger at others, while rarely taking a look at my own sin. Help me to see my sin as You see it, and thus awaken my deep need for Jesus and His redemption. Thank you for the redemptive work He accomplished on the cross. I ask for strength to see others as You see them through the blood of Jesus. I pray these things in Jesus' name, Amen.

Cycle of Praise

"Since what may be known about God is plain to them, because God has made it plain to them. For since the creation of the world God's invisible qualities—his eternal power and divine nature—have been clearly seen, being understood from what has been made, so that people are without excuse.

"For although they knew God, they neither glorified him as God nor gave thanks to him, but their thinking became futile and their foolish hearts were darkened. Although they claimed to be wise, they became fools and exchanged the glory of the immortal God for images made to look like a mortal human being and birds and animals and reptiles." (Romans 1:19-23)

Every human ever created knows of God. Signs of His qualities and attributes are found throughout creation, yet many of us live a lifetime without ever acknowledging God's hand in our lives. You've heard it before: The relieved mother whose kidnapped child was found safe and sound yet responds, "We are so lucky to be together again," the rescued hiker who thanks the men who found and saved her, but fails to recognize God's sovereign role in her recovery, or the burn victim who miraculously escapes from a burning building yet is blind to the miracle God performed in opening a clear path out.   "I am so lucky to be alive."

Paul says that God's "eternal power and divine nature" is clearly seen from creation, so we are without excuse.

It may be easy for us to acknowledge God in the above circumstances, but what about in the little areas? Thanking God when we find a parking spot, when there's food in our 'frig or a warm bed in which to sleep takes effort. These are things we take for granted, yet God wants us to thank Him and glorify Him as Lord of all, even of the little things. This God-focus leads to wisdom, which allows us to see more of His hand in our lives.

Thanking and glorifying God is the beginning of a cycle of praise.

Thank God

Receive Wisdom

Recognize more of God's Work

How often do you recognize the hand of God in your everyday life?

Fifty Two Days of Grace

Do you ever take the little things for granted? Why not take the opportunity right now to thank God for all the little blessings in your life?

Heavenly Father,
I confess that I do not always acknowledge the work of Your hand in my life. I want to thank You for all that You have created, and all the details to which You pay attention, allowing my life to continue. I want to see more of Your hand in my life so I can spend my time praising You!
In Jesus' Name I pray,
Amen

Fifty Two Days of Grace

Doomed for Destruction

"...since what may be known about God is plain to them, because God has made it plain to them. For since the creation of the world God's invisible qualities -- his eternal power and divine nature -- have been clearly seen, being understood from what has been made, so that people are without excuse.

"For although they knew God, they neither glorified him as God nor gave thanks to him, but their thinking became futile and their foolish hearts were darkened. Although they claimed to be wise, they became fools and exchanged the glory of the immortal God for images made to look like a mortal human being and birds and animals and reptiles.

"Therefore God gave them over in the sinful desires of their hearts to sexual impurity for the degrading of their bodies with one another. They exchanged the truth about God for a lie, and worshiped and served created things rather than the Creator—who is forever praised. Amen." (Romans 1:19-25)

"I'll give him exactly what he wants, then we'll see how much he wants it!" cried out the frustrated mom of a willful teenager insisting he would be better off on the street.

Yes, sometimes getting what we asked for backfires because the very thing we think we want is the very thing that brings us down.

Such is the case with our fleshly desires. When we take the God whom we know on a personal level, and replace Him with a desire to please our own flesh and follow our deceitful heart, the result is a downward spiral of destruction that leads away from the Truth.

When in this deluded state, we are helpless to see the truth, similar to the plight of "Ignorance" in John Bunyan's *Pilgrim Progress*. He let his heart lead him away from the truth yet was blissfully ignorant of this reality.

We all want to believe we are basically good, but apart from the redeeming power of Christ, we are doomed for destruction.

Following God's lead, not my heart,
directs me closer to the Truth.

Is there something in your life that you know is not good for you, but you want it anyway? Are you willing to let that thing, person or practice go and surrender it to Jesus?

Do you know the Truth (Jesus Christ is the Way, the Truth and the Life)?

Fifty Two Days of Grace

Are you actively moving toward Jesus? If not, you are drifting away from Him, as if caught in a river current that is taking you downstream, away from Jesus.

Heavenly Father,

Thank you for sending Jesus to take the punishment for my sins, allowing me the privilege to call You Father and spend an eternity with You! I ask for Your strength to sustain me and enable me to continuously move toward You, as if swimming upstream. I desire You above all things.
In Jesus' Name I pray,
Amen.

Fifty Two Days of Grace

Birth of Faith

"You, therefore, have no excuse, you who pass judgment on someone else, for at whatever point you judge another, you are condemning yourself, because you who pass judgment do the same things. Now we know that God's judgment against those who do such things is based on truth. So when you, a mere human being, pass judgment on them and yet do the same things, do you think you will escape God's judgment? Or do you show contempt for the riches of his kindness, forbearance and patience, not realizing that God's kindness is intended to lead you to repentance?" (Romans 2:1-4)

My first daughter was ten days late, and my second pregnancy was high-risk due to triplets, so I spent a lot of time in my young married years waiting around for babies to be born.

The problem is, I am not good at waiting. Maybe I'm just too excited about what I am waiting for to come to fruition, or I could have my own schedule that I expect everyone and everything to heed. Mostly, though, it's just that I don't want to wait. I'd rather things happen right away.

Thankfully, God does not have a problem with waiting for us. In fact, it is part of His character to wait for us to "get it". He is, "not slow in keeping his promise, as some understand slowness" (2 Peter 3:9). He is more concerned with the growth of our hearts than in our schedules, and He is always willing to wait for us to find His way.

When my youngest daughter was learning to sew, there were quite a few times when she had to rip out a seam and start over again. Even though she would rather that it worked right the first time, the detours became a valuable learning opportunity instead of just a frustration.

Just as my periods of waiting ended with the birth of precious lives, God's waiting brings about the birth of faith.

"Biblically, waiting is not just something we have to do until we get what we want. Waiting is part of the process of becoming what God wants us to be."--John Ortberg

Do you accept waiting as a part of your walk with Jesus? If you realized that waiting was beneficial to your faith, how would that improve your attitude?

Name something you have been waiting for, whether it be a loved one to come to Christ, an improvement in the health of a relationship, or something else. How has your heart changed as you've waited?

Heavenly Father,

I thank You for Your patience in waiting for me to understand Your ways and submit myself to You. It is unthinkable that I could be so stubborn and slow! But You are never slow. I ask for help in recognizing the benefits of waiting, and accepting the place in which You

have placed me at this time in my life. I ask for Your blessing on me and my family as we grow in faith.
In Jesus' Name I pray,
Amen

Fifty Two Days of Grace

Hijacked

"You, therefore, have no excuse, you who pass judgment on someone else, for at whatever point you judge another, you are condemning yourself, because you who pass judgment do the same things. Now we know that God's judgment against those who do such things is based on truth. So when you, a mere human being, pass judgment on them and yet do the same things, do you think you will escape God's judgment? Or do you show contempt for the riches of his kindness, forbearance and patience, not realizing that God's kindness is intended to lead you to repentance?" (Romans 2:1-4)

There is a child in one of my Bible classes that continually tries to hijack my class. Even though she is the same age as the other children, she feels the need to chastise them as if she were their mother, rally her classmates to an activity she has decided would be fun at that moment, or tell a story she thinks fits the lesson better than what I have planned. As a teacher, it is frustrating to have a 2nd grader thinking she is better suited than I, an adult, to teach this group of her peers.

We may look at that situation and think how absurd it is for an 8-year-old to teach 2nd graders, yet that is similar to what we do when we judge others. We are in essence saying that we are better suited than God to decide what is right and what is wrong. An absurd and dangerous thought indeed! We, like this young girl, are mere children and are in need of much instruction in the ways of God's Kingdom and in lessons of the heart and are completely unprepared to make this kind of judgment.

It reminds me of the mother who prayed with her children each morning on the way to school. One day the three-year-old prayed, "God, please help Sissy not to suck her thumb." To which Sissy quickly added, "And, God, please help my brother to stop reminding me." Our sin nature begs us to focus on the struggles of those around us, conveniently ignoring the battles right under our own nose.

Pride fools us into believing we are doing pretty good, but boy, does So-and-So need prayer! In reality, we are like David when he was confronted by Nathan of his sin of adultery with Bathsheba. (2 Samuel 12) He didn't recognize his own sin in the scenario Nathan presented to him which clearly illustrated his defiance of God's law. Nathan, the prophet, had to proclaim, "You are the man!" It was not until God had handed down the judgment, however, that David finally "saw the light", repented and fell down on his knees before the Lord.

The truth is that each of us is a sinful human deserving of death, but God in his mercy sent Jesus to make a way for us to enjoy life. We must never forget the kindness, tolerance and patience of God which daily leads us to turn from our sin. Shouldn't we allow this same gift to be given to others, as well?

Judgment of others attempts to hijack God's work of sanctification, while grace points to the cross.

Are you tempted to judge others when you should be shedding light on your own sin?

Do you find it easy to "help" others with their problems, but balk at any attempt others make to shed light on your sin?

How would it change your relationships if you were able to let go of their issues, and instead let God handle it directly with them, absolving you of any responsibility?

Heavenly Father,

Thank You for Your grace and the patience You show in waiting for me to come around to Your ways. I am slow to learn and stubborn to let go of my desires. I ask for help in extending to others the same grace You show me. Please forgive me for the times I have foolishly taken Your place as the one true righteous Judge. May Your Name be glorified in my heart and in my life.
In Jesus' Name I pray,
Amen

Fifty Two Days of Grace

Understand Your Badness

"But because of your stubbornness and your unrepentant heart, you are storing up wrath against yourself for the day of God's wrath, when his righteous judgment will be revealed. God 'will repay each person according to what they have done.' To those who by persistence in doing good seek glory, honor and immortality, he will give eternal life. But for those who are self-seeking and who reject the truth and follow evil, there will be wrath and anger. There will be trouble and distress for every human being who does evil: first for the Jew, then for the Gentile; but glory, honor and peace for everyone who does good: first for the Jew, then for the Gentile. For God does not show favoritism." (Romans 2:5-11)

We live in a world where who we know is more important than what we know. Even a poorly qualified kid with a bad attitude and poor work ethic can get his foot in the door of virtually any corporation or organization with the right connections. It is an attempt to fool Human Resources into thinking this individual would be an asset to their company, and the youngster may even believe that himself.

God is showing us in this passage how different His economy is to the world's. He judges us solely on our heart: our intentions, our attitudes or the direction we turn our face. He knows whether we are seeking our own selfish desires or His. He reads our hearts and identifies whether we follow Him or follow evil. He takes a look at our attitudes and discerns if we have truly accepted the Truth or if we are following a lie. We can't bluff our way past God.

It is easy to read this passage and think, *I'm not following evil. Maybe I'm not fully committed to Jesus, but I'm not evil.* The scriptures tell us differently. Either we are for Him, or against Him. (Matthew 12:30) Either He is master, or something or someone else is. (Matthew 6:24)

Consider the words of C.S. Lewis, author and 20th Century Christian intellectual, "When a man is getting better, he understands more and more clearly the evil that is still left in him. When a man is getting worse, he understands his own badness less and less." Each time we rely on our own judgment of ourselves and our behavior instead of God's, we are following evil.

For example, when I justify the nasty tone when speaking to my husband with the thought that *he deserved that because of how he hurt me this morning,* I am setting my own standards and thus claiming to be my own god. If instead I turn over those feelings of hurt to Jesus and ask Him to show me where I am wrong, I am submitting to His lordship. He will accordingly give me His perspective which sheds light on my own faulty line of reasoning. It is not about being perfect, but about wanting to please my Father more than I want to protect my own feelings. It is about submitting myself to God and letting Him defend me instead of thinking I have to protect myself. This attitude shows how much I trust God.

God isn't impressed with our connections or credentials; we can't fool Him. He is pleased with a heart that is fully committed to Him and a willingness to see our sin for what it is. There is no way to sugar-coat disobedience and rebellion in God's Kingdom.

My heart reveals my motives for which
God will hold me accountable.

How are you guilty of sugar-coating your sin, calling it a "mistake," a "blunder" or an "oversight"?

Are you honest with God, or do you try to bluff your way through prayer, pretending to be something you're not?

Do you believe that God can handle the truth about you, and that He will never forsake you because of the blood of Christ? There is now no condemnation for those who are in Christ Jesus!

Heavenly Father,
I see Your goodness and I know Your standards, yet I try to pretend I'm something I'm not when I'm spending time with You. Thank You for the abundance of Your grace. I ask Your help in dropping the pretenses

and being honest and authentic in my relationship with You. I know You love me with a love that will never end. Help me to accept Your unconditional love.
In Jesus' Name I pray,
Amen

God is our Conscience

"All who sin apart from the law will also perish apart from the law, and all who sin under the law will be judged by the law. For it is not those who hear the law who are righteous in God's sight, but it is those who obey the law who will be declared righteous. (Indeed, when Gentiles, who do not have the law, do by nature things required by the law, they are a law for themselves, even though they do not have the law. They show that the requirements of the law are written on their hearts, their consciences also bearing witness, and their thoughts sometimes accusing them and at other times even defending them.) This will take place on the day when God judges people's secrets through Jesus Christ, as my gospel declares."
(Romans 2:12-16)

"Let your conscience be your guide." Many of us probably remember these words of wisdom given to Pinocchio from Jiminy Cricket, the guide and conscience assigned by the Blue Fairy to the little puppet who wanted to be a real boy. This is a cute children's story and a nice thought, but it's interesting to think about the source of our conscience. This passage shows us that God has ingrained within us a sense of right and wrong based on His standards. There are many external influences which try to change this measure, but deep down, each one of us knows that benchmark. Whether or not we acknowledge it and act according to it is another matter entirely!

Consider the grasp even non-believers have of this reality. Journalist Sydney Harris wrote, "Once we assuage our conscience by calling something a 'necessary evil,' it begins to look more and more necessary and less and less evil." When we begin to walk down that wide path that leads to destruction, it is difficult to turn around and come back to the narrow gate. (Matthew 7:13) But come back, we must! James 1:22 reminds us that we are required to obey this Word that is written on our hearts, not just listen to it; and here is where the challenge begins.

Following God's code that is written on our hearts may be difficult at times, but it is not without reason. It reminds me of the story I heard of a man who built his own house in Florida. When Hurricane Andrew came barreling through in 1992, his house was the only one left standing in his neighborhood. The reason? He strictly followed the Florida state building code, which is designed so houses could withstand hurricanes. It worked! Similarly, when we follow God's ways, and let our conscience be our guide, we will withstand the pressures of this world.

Following God's laws can help us withstand the storms of life, and leave us standing in the end.

When do you ignore your conscience, thus ignoring God?

How can you purpose to spend more time studying God's Word and applying it to your life?

It is hard to do what God says, especially when it goes against your natural tendencies. Which area of your life can you begin to obey God in today?

Heavenly Father,

I praise You for I am fearfully and wonderfully made! You have taken such care in creating me, even going so far as to write Your word on my heart. I ask for Your help as I try to listen to Your voice, and obey what it says. I want to take Your laws seriously, knowing that You created them for a purpose.
I pray these things in Jesus' name,
Amen

Fifty Two Days of Grace

Don't You Know Who I Am?

"Now you, if you call yourself a Jew; if you rely on the law and boast in God; if you know his will and approve of what is superior because you are instructed by the law; if you are convinced that you are a guide for the blind, a light for those who are in the dark, an instructor of the foolish, a teacher of little children, because you have in the law the embodiment of knowledge and truth— you, then, who teach others, do you not teach yourself? You who preach against stealing, do you steal? You who say that people should not commit adultery, do you commit adultery? You who abhor idols, do you rob temples? You who boast in the law, do you dishonor God by breaking the law? As it is written: 'God's name is blasphemed among the Gentiles because of you.'

"Circumcision has value if you observe the law, but if you break the law, you have become as though you had not been circumcised. So then, if those who are not circumcised keep the law's requirements, will they not be regarded as though they were circumcised? The one who is not circumcised physically and yet obeys the law will condemn you who, even though you have the written code and circumcision, are a lawbreaker.

"A person is not a Jew who is one only outwardly, nor is circumcision merely outward and physical." (Romans 2:17-28)

A few years ago, the Lieutenant Governor in our state was caught speeding on the freeway in excess of 100 miles-per-hour. When the State Patrolman pulled him over, this arrogant man asked, "Don't you know who I am?" The officer then let him off with a warning instead of issuing a ticket according to procedure. This mentality of being above the law is rampant in today's political system, but it is also an attitude we as believers must guard against.

It is surprising how often the attitude that we have an inside track with God rears its ugly head. Whenever we look at all the things we do for His Kingdom, and then justify ourselves based on our own standards, we place ourselves on thin ice. With this superior outlook, we are unable to meet anyone where they are. Instead, we have placed ourselves in a position above them. What we must remember is that God doesn't need us to accomplish His will, it is only because of God's grace that we have been called to any particular ministry or station in life, and every gift we have comes from our Father. Nothing depends on us, but on the working of God's Spirit in our lives and in the lives of those around us. In this light, our position is humbled and we are better able to love the people God has put in our lives.

There once was a CEO of a large company who was standing in line at the DMV. He grumbled to his wife, "Don't they know who I am?" To which she replied, "Yeah, you're a plumber's son who got lucky." Each one of us is a sinner plucked from the claws of death by a Savior who presents us before the Lord as a gleaming, white saint. Remembering who we really are, not who our ego says we are, is vital to keeping a humble manner. But perhaps English writer G.K. Chesterton said it best when he claimed, "All men are ordinary men; the extraordinary men are those who know it."

> *It's not our stature that counts, but the state of our heart that really matters*

How do you think of yourself more highly than you ought?

How does remembering who you are in Christ help to humble you?

Without Christ, you are nothing. Is this something you have accepted in your heart, or do you still hold onto the belief that there is a little bit of good in you?

Heavenly Father,

Thank You for the gracious gift of Jesus that enables us to have a relationship with You. I ask for forgiveness for my prideful attitude and ask for Your help in humbling myself before You, remembering my place. Even though I may think I'm something extra special, I need to recognize that my worth comes from You and I am nothing without the blood of Jesus.
I pray these things in Jesus' Name, Amen

Fifty Two Days of Grace

Birthright

"Now you, if you call yourself a Jew; if you rely on the law and boast in God; if you know his will and approve of what is superior because you are instructed by the law; if you are convinced that you are a guide for the blind, a light for those who are in the dark, an instructor of the foolish, a teacher of little children, because you have in the law the embodiment of knowledge and truth— you, then, who teach others, do you not teach yourself? You who preach against stealing, do you steal? You who say that people should not commit adultery, do you commit adultery? You who abhor idols, do you rob temples? You who boast in the law, do you dishonor God by breaking the law? As it is written: 'God's name is blasphemed among the Gentiles because of you.'

"Circumcision has value if you observe the law, but if you break the law, you have become as though you had not been circumcised. So then, if those who are not circumcised keep the law's requirements, will they not be regarded as though they were circumcised? The one who is not circumcised physically and yet obeys the law will condemn you who, even though you have the written code and circumcision, are a lawbreaker.

"A person is not a Jew who is one only outwardly, nor is circumcision merely outward and physical." (Romans 2:17-28)

The other day I was working late and my daughter was making dinner. When it was ready, she called the whole family and we gathered around the table, enjoying the food and each other's company. It struck me that I had not lifted a finger to make the delectable meal, but I was enjoying the fruits of my daughter's labor simply because I was a part of the family. My family connection bought me a ticket to that fine feast.

Sometimes we take on this same expectation regarding salvation. We think if we were born into a Christian family, we are automatically invited to dine at the table of salvation. Paul teaches us in Galatians 6:15 that circumcision, or birthright, no longer buys us a spot in God's family. Instead, it is a simple faith in Jesus Christ that inducts us into His family.

Billy Sunday, Evangelist of the early 20th Century, knew this truth only too well. Despite the fact that he had led thousands of people to Christ, his own sons remained lost. Their birth into the family of a man whom God used to impact so many did nothing for their own salvation. They were not automatically adopted into God's family by their birthright. Instead, they had to repent and trust in Jesus, just like everyone else. There is no special privilege in the kingdom of God!

If you think you are part of the family of God because you were born into a church-going family, or do all the things you think God wants you to do like attend Bible study and serve others, remember the words of preacher and writer Vance Havner. He said, "You can become a Christian by going to church just about as easily as you can become an automobile by sleeping in a garage." Don't rely on your family heritage or your outward works. Taste the Lord for yourself and see that He is good! (Psalm 34:8)

> "...confess with your mouth, 'Jesus is Lord' and
> believe in your heart that God raised him from
> the dead, you will be saved." (Romans 10:9)

Have you trusted Jesus as your personal Lord and Savior?

Do you spend time in quiet study, reflection and meditation on God's Word, helping you to better get to know your Savior?

Heavenly Father,
I praise You for Your gift of salvation through faith in Jesus Christ. Because of this overwhelming gift, anyone has a chance to live with You forever. Sometimes I take this act of grace for granted and keep You at a distance, assuming that going to church will save me. I ask for strength to be able to stick with my daily time with You; I want to know You more!
In Jesus' Name I pray,
Amen

Fifty Two Days of Grace

Branded by Love

"Now you, if you call yourself a Jew; if you rely on the law and boast in God; if you know his will and approve of what is superior because you are instructed by the law; if you are convinced that you are a guide for the blind, a light for those who are in the dark, an instructor of the foolish, a teacher of little children, because you have in the law the embodiment of knowledge and truth— you, then, who teach others, do you not teach yourself? You who preach against stealing, do you steal? You who say that people should not commit adultery, do you commit adultery? You who abhor idols, do you rob temples? You who boast in the law, do you dishonor God by breaking the law? As it is written: 'God's name is blasphemed among the Gentiles because of you.'

"Circumcision has value if you observe the law, but if you break the law, you have become as though you had not been circumcised. So then, if those who are not circumcised keep the law's requirements, will they not be regarded as though they were circumcised? The one who is not circumcised physically and yet obeys the law will condemn you who, even though you have the written code and circumcision, are a lawbreaker.

"A person is not a Jew who is one only outwardly, nor is circumcision merely outward and physical." (Romans 2:17-28)

Driving into a local Walmart parking lot the other day, I found myself behind an old station wagon that was plastered with bumper stickers declaring the driver's belief in Christ as his Savior. I had not even finished taking in all the messages when, completely contrary to what I had been reading, this man cut off another driver who had been waiting for a parking spot and then shook his fist out the window at the dismayed woman! His actions did not live up to the messages he proclaimed so loudly on the back end of his car.

Jesus said we would be known by our love. There is no need to circumcise or mark ourselves as believers because He has circumcised our hearts. People will recognize us not by our outward appearance or by the messages we proclaim on the back of our vehicles, but by the patient and kind way we treat each other, in the way we forgive, or in the way we never give up on anyone no matter how many times they hurt us. God's love flowing through us will make us stand out like a beacon from the rest of the world. No bumper sticker can do that!

Scottish theologian and author William Barclay is credited with the following wisdom. "More people have been brought into the church by the kindness of real Christian love than by all the theological arguments in the world, and more people have been driven from the church by the hardness and ugliness of so-called Christianity than by all the doubts in the world." God's love does what no amount of well-crafted sermons, intellectual discussions or persuasive arguments can do: It breaks through a hard shell, mends a broken heart and draws a fearful soul. By giving people a glimpse of that thing for which they have been searching but didn't, until that moment, know its identity, we are letting God use us to proclaim the gospel in a concrete and practical way.

The words of Jesus recorded in John 13:34 tell us that we would be recognized as His disciples if we love one another. Love is our brand; not a symbol, slogan or way of speaking. Simply love.

Let the way you love others speak for itself.

When do you try to depend upon outward appearances to identify yourself as belonging to Christ?

How do you attempt to prove your allegiance to Christ in word and deed instead of letting Him rule your heart?

Heavenly Father,

I praise You for the unspeakable love You have perfectly shown me through Your Son Jesus Christ. Please forgive me for trying to artificially brand myself as Yours but instead help me to place my life into Your hands for Your purposes. In this way, people will recognize Your love as it flows through me.
In Jesus' Name I pray,
Amen

Fifty Two Days of Grace

Our Advantage

"What advantage, then, is there in being a Jew, or what value is there in circumcision? Much in every way! First of all, the Jews have been entrusted with the very words of God. What if some were unfaithful? Will their unfaithfulness nullify God's faithfulness? Not at all! Let God be true, and every human being a liar. As it is written: 'So that you may be proved right when you speak and prevail when you judge.'" (Romans 3:1-4)

There are many religions man uses to try to get to God. Each has its own list of requirements to fulfill in order for a follower to climb closer to the ultimate goal. Each uses a standard set by man to measure a disciple's progress and many followers claim to have found peace and meaning in this process.

So what advantage do we, as disciples of Christ, hold? We have the very words of God to use as our blueprint for building a meaningful life and to employ as a standard with which to measure our hearts. Many times we fail to use God's Word in this way, but simply read it as part of a ritual or as a daily habit. The amazing thing about God, is that this lack of faith on our part does not at all change His character. If I claim that the maple tree in my front yard does not exist, that does not make it true, as evidenced by the shade I enjoy in the summer or the leaves I rake up each fall. The tree is there no matter what I believe in my heart about it or how many times I ignore it as I walk past it on the way to the car. In the same way, God's faithfulness to fulfill his promises and to love us as only He can is not invalidated by my "lukewarmness." If I simply go through the motions of doing "religious things", but make no real investment in my relationship with my Father, it does not diminish one iota His character. He is still the same today as He was when He created all things. (Psalm 102:25-27)

Knowing that God is there waiting for me to place Him in the center of my life, and that He won't be a different God once I finally appreciate and acknowledge Him is comforting and inspiring. I want to know a God who doesn't change! Everything else around me is constantly changing: my relationships, my family, my garden, my home, my job. Nothing stays the same. Nothing, that is, except God. That is our advantage as the people of the One True God.

When all else is shifting, I can
hang on to the Solid Rock.

When do I expect God to change with the times?

How do I live a life devoid of contact with my Father who loves me perfectly?

Fifty Two Days of Grace

Heavenly Father,

I praise You for being a God who never changes. Due to Your steady, rock-solid character, I can trust You in all things and at all times. Forgive me for not always acknowledging You as sovereign over my life. Thank You for Your patience as You wait for me to place You at the center of my life, where You belong. I find it remarkable that You don't give up on me.

In Jesus' Name I pray,

Amen

Fifty Two Days of Grace

Calvary's Triumph

"'Their feet are swift to shed blood; ruin and misery mark their ways, and the way of peace they do not know.' 'There is no fear of God before their eyes.'

"Now we know that whatever the law says, it says to those who are under the law, so that every mouth may be silenced and the whole world held accountable to God. Therefore no one will be declared righteous in God's sight by the works of the law; rather, through the law we become conscious of our sin." (Romans 3:15-20)

A few years ago I made a list on a poster of some of the laws found in the Old Testament. I was attempting to illustrate to a class of elementary and middle school students the futility of trying to earn my righteousness by following the rules God gave us to outline His high standards for living. As we went down the list, we talked about whether or not we had completely obeyed that law 100% of the time, which is His expectation for us. If we were honest with ourselves, we admitted we were utter failures in living our lives to God's standard. How hopeless we felt and how powerless against our flesh and in our ability to do the right thing we discovered we were.

If that was the end of the story, we would all be without hope indeed. But that is not the end, in fact that is only the beginning. The law only exists to show us where we need a Savior to bridge the gap between our imperfection and God's perfection, between our wretchedness and God's holiness, between our inadequacy and God's sufficiency. And Jesus is that Savior!

Preacher Larry McGuill spoke to the importance of putting our trust in Jesus, not in our own efforts of following the law. He said, "It is the rightful heritage of every believer, even the newest in the family of faith, to be absolutely certain that eternal life is his present possession. To look to self is to tremble. To look to Calvary's finished work is triumph."

We can stand as victors in the battle Christ waged against sin on our behalf. As recipients of this unspeakable gift of salvation, we are called to live as conquerors. We are not called to try to be perfect in an effort to impress God and others with our righteousness. Instead, we are called to submit ourselves to our Father's will, knowing He has already accepted us as His children, made perfect by the blood of His Son. The battle against the power of sin is already won!

Following the Law is Futile, Following
the Savior offers Freedom

How often do you attempt to meet God's standard of perfection in an attempt to win God's favor?

Fifty Two Days of Grace

Do you find yourself feeling guilty for failing or for not being what you think is good enough in God's eyes?

How do you forget the triumph over sin Jesus secured for you on the cross at Calvary?

Heavenly Father,
Jesus paid the ultimate price when He gave His life as a ransom for mine, purchasing my freedom from the bondage of sin. Help me to live my life as a conqueror, tasting the full and meaningful life Jesus came to give me.
In Jesus' name I pray,
Amen

Fifty Two Days of Grace

God's Favor

"Therefore no one will be declared righteous in God's sight by the works of the law; rather, through the law we become conscious of our sin. But now apart from the law the righteousness of God has been made known, to which the Law and the Prophets testify. This righteousness is given through faith in Jesus Christ to all who believe. There is no difference between Jew and Gentile, for all have sinned and fall short of the glory of God, and all are justified freely by his grace through the redemption that came by Christ Jesus. God presented Christ as a sacrifice of atonement, through the shedding of his blood—to be received by faith. He did this to demonstrate his righteousness, because in his forbearance he had left the sins committed beforehand unpunished— he did it to demonstrate his righteousness at the present time, so as to be just and the one who justifies those who have faith in Jesus."
(Romans 3:20-26)

Recently, I have become friends with a lovely Muslim woman in my neighborhood. As we share with each other about cooking, gardening, mothering and our faith, I am struck by the Muslim belief that Allah will judge her on judgment day according to her good and bad works. She says only Allah knows whether one will go to heaven or hell, and she won't find out until that day.

Consequently, Muslims put a lot of emphasis on following their laws. They must use their own judgment to decide what is important to Allah and do those things in order to win his favor. It seems like a hopeless and discouraging way to live.

In contrast, we are not bound by these same restrictions. Followers of Christ are not made righteous by our deeds, but through faith in Jesus Christ. It is impossible for us to be made righteous through works, because we all fall short of God's standard. Unfortunately, it is human nature for us to use God's Word as a litmus test, or a ruler by which we measure our life or the lives of other believers. When we do this, we are reverting to the old covenant by which the blood of sacrificed animals partially, but not fully, atoned for our sins. Thankfully, under the new covenant, the blood of Jesus provides complete atonement for all who believe. God's justice has already been demonstrated through the sacrifice of Christ, The Lamb of God. There is no need for us to put our trust in the law to save us, as the Muslims do.

Writer Mark Twain humorously explains God's gift of salvation this way. "Heaven goes by favor. If it went by merit, you would stay out, and your dog would go in." Dogs are much better natured than humans in many ways, but we are made in God's image and have been given the gift of salvation through the faith in our Lord and Savior, Jesus Christ. Let us not fall into the trap of judging ourselves or others by works, as those who follow other gods do. Instead, let us rest in the assurance of our Savior's redemptive work on the cross.

"For it is by grace you have been saved, through faith — and this not from yourselves, it is the gift of God — not by works, so that no one can boast." (Ephesians 2:8-9)

When do you attempt to judge yourself based on the standard you think God holds for you?

How do you minimize the redemptive work of Christ on the cross in the way you try to be saved by your actions and behavior?

Heavenly Father,

Thank You for sending Jesus to take the punishment meant for my sins. Since I am judged solely based on what Jesus has already done, I can rest assured that my salvation is secured. Help me to live my life in the freedom found in the blood of Jesus.
In Jesus' name I pray,
Amen

Fifty Two Days of Grace

God-Generated

"Where, then, is boasting? It is excluded. Because of what law? The law that requires works? No, because of the law that requires faith. For we maintain that a person is justified by faith apart from the works of the law. Or is God the God of Jews only? Is he not the God of Gentiles too? Yes, of Gentiles too, since there is only one God, who will justify the circumcised by faith and the uncircumcised through that same faith. Do we, then, nullify the law by this faith? Not at all! Rather, we uphold the law." (Romans 3:27-31)

Many of us are stuck on the law. We can't get away from the habit of depending on our own effort to look godly. Jesus, however, represents a new way. Through His sacrifice on the cross, He made a way for us to enjoy a personal relationship with God. Within the boundaries of this relationship, we learn to follow Him as a lamb would follow its shepherd. A shepherd would never lead his flock into danger. In the same way, Jesus will never lead us down a path that would break the law.

In the old covenant, God's people had to follow the law. When they inevitably broke the law, they were required to make a blood sacrifice in order to atone for that sin. It was an endless cycle. Under the new covenant, Jesus took all our sin upon Himself and became the final, perfect sacrifice, opening up a whole new way of interacting with God. We are now able to follow Him personally, leading us to uphold His law and thus glorify God. This is not to say we are perfect and never fall, but that we are able, through His Spirit living within us, to live godly lives. In this way we glorify God.

It reminds me of the drive-in restaurant in Southern California where a dozen hand-lettered signs were seen displayed in various places informing customers of what the owner required them to do and forbid them not to do. To say the least, this was not a pleasant place to dine. We can no more comprehend and obey all of God's laws than those diners can follow all the owner required, but we can follow God who will never lead us wrong!

Everything we do must be God-generated.

When do you live by the sweat of your own brow, trying to gain God's favor in the way you obey His law?

How would following Jesus instead of His law transform the way you feel about your life?

Heavenly Father,
Thank You for sending Jesus to set me free from the law of sin and death. Now, instead of worrying how many times I fail or how far I fall short, I can enjoy You as I live in relationship with You. Without the sacrifice Jesus made on the cross, I would never have the

opportunity to know You so intimately. Help me to never forget this benefit.
In Jesus' Name I pray,
Amen

Fifty Two Days of Grace

The Chair

"What then shall we say that Abraham, our forefather according to the flesh, discovered in this matter? If, in fact, Abraham was justified by works, he had something to boast about—but not before God. What does Scripture say? 'Abraham believed God, and it was credited to him as righteousness.' Now to the one who works, wages are not credited as a gift but as an obligation. However, to the one who does not work but trusts God who justifies the ungodly, their faith is credited as righteousness. David says the same thing when he speaks of the blessedness of the one to whom God credits righteousness apart from works: 'Blessed are those whose transgressions are forgiven, whose sins are covered. Blessed is the one whose sin the Lord will never count against them.'

"Is this blessedness only for the circumcised, or also for the uncircumcised? We have been saying that Abraham's faith was credited to him as righteousness. Under what circumstances was it credited? Was it after he was circumcised, or before? It was not after, but before! And he received circumcision as a sign, a seal of the righteousness that he had by faith while he was still uncircumcised. So then, he is the father of all who believe but have not been circumcised, in order that righteousness might be credited to them. And he is then also the father of

the circumcised who not only are circumcised but who also follow in the footsteps of the faith that our father Abraham had before he was circumcised." (Romans 4:1-12)

"Now faith is being sure of what we hope for and certain of what we do not see." (Hebrews 11:1)

Jesus, being the author and perfecter of our faith, has equipped us to trust God for our justification. No one that ever lived has been successful to work his way into God's graces. Even Abraham, who was considered to be a friend of God and made it into the -- Hall of Fame of Faith -- found in Hebrews 11, was made righteous not by his effort, but by his belief in God.

When we refrain from working to try to get right with God but instead trust simply in Him, the dividend of this faith is righteousness. We can't trust God without faith in Him, and we can't be made righteous without trusting God. Trust is the manifestation of our faith. We know we have faith in God when we act on that faith by obeying His calling, just like Abraham did many times.

Think about a chair. Before we sit down, we have to have faith that the chair will do as it promises to do; hold our full weight without collapsing. We put that faith to the test by trusting this chair with our load, and thus lowering ourselves down to rest in it. The act of sitting would never occur if we didn't trust the chair, and we'd never trust the chair if we didn't have faith in its integrity, character and ability to deliver on its promise to hold us. Likewise, action (obedience) is the evidence of trusting God, but trusting is impossible without faith in Him. This faith in action results in the gift of righteousness, something that can never be earned in our own effort.

When we show our faith in God,
we are made sinless in His eyes.

How do you try to earn your righteousness by doing good deeds?

When do you feel so unworthy of God's love that you keep your distance in shame?

Heavenly Father,
Thank You for Your unspeakable love. This amazing love sent Jesus to the cross, taking the punishment meant for my sins and thus making a way for me to get right with You. Help me to treasure this bond that has been created between us by the blood of Jesus, holding it as my most treasured possession. Every time I trust You enough to live as You intended me to live, I am using the gift of faith You have provided.
In Jesus' Name I pray,
Amen

Fifty Two Days of Grace

Nothing

"As it is written: 'I have made you a father of many nations.' He is our father in the sight of God, in whom he believed—the God who gives life to the dead and calls into being things that were not." (Romans 4:17)

I recently was reminiscing about my 25th High School Reunion. These events can be quite interesting and revealing. There are those expected outcomes like the yearbook editor who works as a successful reporter, or the good student and popular quarterback who now thrives as a dentist and politician. But then there are the surprises, like the class clown and "D" student who prospers as a chiropractor or the shy wall flower who became a vocal advocate for battered women. These are unexpected developments.

This is how God likes to work. He chooses the foolish, weak and lowly things of this world to shame the wise, strong and lofty. Why does He do this? To build up our "self-confidence" or give us a sense of purpose for our otherwise dreary lives? No! He operates in this backward fashion so that none of us can boast before Him. (I Corinthians 1:27-29) He pours the richness of His Spirit into our fragile forms in order to make us humble and to ensure that He gets all the honor and glory. It's so easy for us humans to get too big for our britches.

We enjoy a success and then tend to drift toward thoughts of self-congratulations.

The reality is, however, that God can use even stones to praise Him! (Luke 19:40) God doesn't need us or our qualifications or gifts to bring praise and glory to Himself: He can just as easily use a rock.

> *"Until a man is nothing, God can make nothing out of him."*…Martin Luther

When do you assume that you must be someone important in order to be used by God?

How do you resist the work of God in your life because you can't get over yourself?

Heavenly Father,

Thank You for choosing me because of Your great love for me; nothing more. May my life bring honor and glory to You as I commit myself into Your hands. Help me to always remember and appreciate how You are in the business of taking nothing and making it into something.

In Jesus' Name I pray,

Amen

Hope against all hope

"Against all hope, Abraham in hope believed and so became the father of many nations, just as it had been said to him, 'So shall your offspring be.' Without weakening in his faith, he faced the fact that his body was as good as dead—since he was about a hundred years old—and that Sarah's womb was also dead. Yet he did not waver through unbelief regarding the promise of God, but was strengthened in his faith and gave glory to God, being fully persuaded that God had power to do what he had promised."
(Romans 4:18-21)

Hope can be defined as "a sure and steady faith in God's promises." Hope has sustained people through many difficult times. It gave Corrie Ten Boom the will to continue living in a Nazi Concentration Camp even when her beloved sister died, knowing that they would again be together in eternity. Hope gave a missionary the strength to carry on in a hostile environment, knowing that, "my word that goes out from my mouth; it will not return to me empty, but will accomplish what I desire and achieve the purpose for which I sent it." (Isaiah 55:11) And hope gave Abraham the ability to believe, against all odds, that he and his wife Sarah would become parents in their old age. Abraham overlooked the physical confirmation of his inabilities, choosing to believe that God had the power to fulfill his promises. This is the basis of hope: Believing that God is able to do what He said He would do despite the evidence that seems to indicate otherwise.

Where do you need a dose of hope? In the hospital waiting room? In the bitter relationship with your spouse? Beside the grave of your beloved? In your dead-end job? On the threshold of an uncertain future? When things seem hopeless? Through faith in Jesus Christ, we have the hope of an eternity with Him. And perhaps more powerful than that, we have the hope of a life made meaningful through our intimate relationship with the One who created us for a specific purpose and who loves us beyond measure.

Faith is using hope to believe
when it seems there is no hope.

When do you give up as soon as circumstances seem insurmountable?

How can you bolster your faith in times when things look hopeless?

Heavenly Father,
I praise You for being a God who gives me all the hope I need to keep going. Instead of focusing on the physical facts around me, help me to fix my attention on You, the One who never fails and who always loves.
In Jesus' Name I pray, Amen

Diametrically Opposed

"Since we have now been justified by his blood, how much more shall we be saved from God's wrath through him! For if, while we were God's enemies, we were reconciled to him through the death of his Son, how much more, having been reconciled, shall we be saved through his life! Not only is this so, but we also boast in God through our Lord Jesus Christ, through whom we have now received reconciliation." (Romans 5:9-11)

Enemy. The word conjures up images of Osama bin Laden, or Adolf Hitler. It also brings to mind enemies of classic fictional characters: Batman and the Joker, Superman and Lex Luthor, Tweety Bird and Sylvester the Cat. One thing that does not come to mind when we hear the word "enemy," however, is ourselves and God. But that is what Paul tells us in Romans 5:10; because of our sin, we were God's enemies. Webster defines an enemy as, "one who is antagonistic to another." In our sin, we are in opposition to God and are at odds with Him and His message.

I don't know about you, but I don't like to think of myself as being against God. I want to think that I am a pretty decent person and that I would not do anything counter to God's ways. But the truth is that we are anything but a friend of

God. We are His foe. In order to be reconciled to our Creator we all need a mediator: Someone to reconcile us with a perfect and holy God to whom we are diametrically opposed.

I can't think of anyone who could have reconciled a relationship between Osama bin Laden and the United States. His entire being was against our beliefs, values and norms. But this is similar to what Jesus Christ did for us when dying on the cross for our punishment: He bridged the chasm between our sinful selves and a holy God. By accepting God's free gift of salvation, through faith in Jesus, we are reconciled with God and can now be considered as His friends. We can "rejoice in God through our Lord Jesus Christ, through whom we have now received reconciliation". (Romans 5:11) Jesus accomplished through his death that which none of us have any hope of doing on our own: he turned enemies into friends.

Rejoice! Through faith in Jesus Christ,
we are no longer God's enemies.

What does it mean to you that you are naturally an enemy of God?

How are you taking advantage of the friendship that has been made possible between you and God through faith in Jesus Christ?

Fifty Two Days of Grace

Heavenly Father,

I praise You for the relationship I can now enjoy with You through faith in Jesus Christ. What a joy it is for me, a natural enemy, to be able to boldly approach Your throne of grace. Help me to always stay close to You and take full advantage of the benefits that are mine through faith in Christ.

In Jesus' Name I pray,

Amen

Fifty Two Days of Grace

God's Call

"You see, at just the right time, when we were still powerless, Christ died for the ungodly. Very rarely will anyone die for a righteous person, though for a good person someone might possibly dare to die. But God demonstrates his own love for us in this: While we were still sinners, Christ died for us.

"Since we have now been justified by his blood, how much more shall we be saved from God's wrath through him!" (Romans 5:6-9)

I remember hearing the report of a woman who had been attacked by a cougar while out hiking. Left to die, she crawled her way back to her car. Meanwhile, rescuers searched for her and found her in the nick of time to save her life, when she was most in need.

Jesus has this kind of timing, "...at just the right time, while we were still powerless, Christ died for the ungodly." (v 6) God's timing was perfect. He sent Jesus when we were "utterly helpless." (NLT) I believe this is the pattern for salvation, as well. Jesus doesn't want us to wait until we have our act together before we come to Him. He wants us to come to Him as we are; broken, powerless and helpless. That is the perfect time to accept the gift of salvation: while we recognize our sin. We can't wait until we think we've got everything under control and are cleaned up and presentable. It will then be too late because we won't see our need for a Savior.

God's call is never too late, so
drop everything to respond.

Have you accepted God's free gift of salvation that comes through faith in Jesus Christ? If not, what are you waiting for?

When do you put pressure on yourself to meet a standard that is impossible to reach?

Heavenly Father,
I praise You for Your perfect timing. Even though I am tempted to clean myself up as to appear more presentable before I invite You into my life, I know You'd rather take me just as I am. Thank you for loving me enough to meet me where I am, and help me to love others in the same way.
In Jesus' Name I pray,
Amen

Truth

"Therefore, just as sin entered the world through one man, and death through sin, and in this way death came to all people, because all sinned—

"To be sure, sin was in the world before the law was given, but sin is not charged against anyone's account where there is no law. Nevertheless, death reigned from the time of Adam to the time of Moses, even over those who did not sin by breaking a command, as did Adam, who is a pattern of the one to come.

"But the gift is not like the trespass. For if the many died by the trespass of the one man, how much more did God's grace and the gift that came by the grace of the one man, Jesus Christ, overflow to the many! Nor can the gift of God be compared with the result of one man's sin: The judgment followed one sin and brought condemnation, but the gift followed many trespasses and brought justification. For if, by the trespass of the one man, death reigned through that one man, how much more will those who receive God's abundant provision of grace and of the gift of righteousness reign in life through the one man, Jesus Christ!

"Consequently, just as one trespass resulted in condemnation for all people, so also one righteous act resulted in justification and life for all people. For just as through the disobedience of the one man the many were made sinners, so also through the obedience of the one man the many will be made righteous.

"The law was brought in so that the trespass might increase. But where sin increased, grace increased all the more, so that, just as sin reigned in death, so also grace might reign through righteousness to bring eternal life through Jesus Christ our Lord." (Romans 5:12-21)

Winston Churchill said, "Men stumble over the truth from time to time, but most pick themselves up and hurry off as if nothing happened." The Truth that is Jesus Christ is meant to change us, to impact our lives in such a way that we are forever different in our thinking and acting. Unfortunately, as Churchill so aptly pointed out, this rarely happens.

I have a friend who believes all religions are the same, all beliefs are equally true. She and her husband teach their family of eight children to embrace all beliefs, but choose none as the truth. This is a very convenient way to think, because the implication is that if there is no right, then there is no wrong. There is no judgment. There is no sin. We can all live our lives according to our own standards, and therefore think we are doing pretty well. We're not so bad, after all. But God's Word teaches differently. In Romans 5:12, Paul tells us that sin entered the world through Adam, and through this sin we are all condemned to death. The good news is that in the same way, grace overflows to many through Jesus: One Man, one Truth.

Fifty Two Days of Grace

What worries me about my friend's belief system is that she is fooling herself into thinking she is free from the restraints of any particular religion. Unfortunately, she is wrong. She is bound to the condemnation of sin, whether she believes it or not. But grace is available through One Man. May this Truth set her free!

The truth is right in front of us, if only we could see then we would have eternal life, and finally be set free.

When do you bend the truth to fit your own way of living?

How are you living a lie that conveniently paints yourself in a rosy light?

Heavenly Father,
Thank You for making the truth clear and easily discernible. Even though the truth of the Gospel may not always be easy to accept, I am grateful for the clear boundaries set forth in Your Word. Help me to live according to this Truth all the days of my life, remembering that I am a sinner saved by grace.
In Jesus' Name I pray,
Amen

Fifty Two Days of Grace

The Great Exchange

"What shall we say, then? Shall we go on sinning so that grace may increase? By no means! We are those who have died to sin; how can we live in it any longer? Or don't you know that all of us who were baptized into Christ Jesus were baptized into his death? We were therefore buried with him through baptism into death in order that, just as Christ was raised from the dead through the glory of the Father, we too may live a new life." (Romans 6:1-4)

Young children constantly test their parents' authority to see if it is present. If Dad says, "Don't touch," the toddler may touch just the forbidden object to see what her dad will do. If Mom says, "Don't run," the pre-schooler may run to find out what happens. Once a child reaches a certain age, however, he knows whether or not his parents hold the authority and if they are willing to back it up.

If Paul's letter to the Romans tells us that the law is dead and we are saved by grace, should we test God and continue to live in sin to see if grace really does save us in the end? Or let one area of sin flourish so others know we are not perfect, thus showcasing God's wonderful grace in our lives so everyone can see the kind of God we serve?

Absolutely not! We are dead to sin, it no longer has a hold on us. We have another option other than giving in to our flesh, and that is to surrender our sins to Jesus. He already bore them in death so that we might live for righteousness (I Peter 2:24). There is no need for us to test Him on this mystery, as Martin Luther labeled it. "This is the mystery of the riches of divine grace for sinners, for by a wonderful exchange our sins are now not ours but Christ's, and Christ's righteousness is not Christ's, but ours."

Participate in the great exchange,
and test the Lord no more

When do you unknowingly test the Lord and His willingness to forgive your sins?

How are you living the life of the unsaved instead of putting on the cloak of righteousness Jesus so graciously bought with His blood?

Heavenly Father,
You have paid for my righteousness through the precious blood of Your Son. Help me to remember this great exchange where my sin is exchanged for Christ's righteousness and live in a way that honors such a sacrifice. I am forever grateful for this unimaginable gift of grace.
In Jesus' Name I pray,
Amen

Instruments of Righteousness

"For if we have been united with him in a death like his, we will certainly also be united with him in a resurrection like his. For we know that our old self was crucified with him so that the body ruled by sin might be done away with, that we should no longer be slaves to sin — because anyone who has died has been set free from sin.

"Now if we died with Christ, we believe that we will also live with him. For we know that since Christ was raised from the dead, he cannot die again; death no longer has mastery over him. The death he died, he died to sin once for all; but the life he lives, he lives to God.

"In the same way, count yourselves dead to sin but alive to God in Christ Jesus."
(Romans 6:5-11)

In J.R.R. Tolkien's epic *Lord of the Rings*, Frodo is given the task of transporting the powerful ring to its birthplace where it can then be destroyed. Along the way, Aragorn gives him a small sword as a weapon of defense. I always thought, *what good is that wimpy thing going to do against the likes of Sauron and his Ringwraiths?*

It's the same with us and sin. What good is our own wimpy effort against the power of sin in our lives? Thankfully, God has given us a powerful weapon in Jesus Christ. We are dead to sin and alive to God in Christ Jesus. (Romans 6:11) Sin no longer has to be our master because we are under grace. Grace is like our weapon against sin. By God's grace through faith in Jesus Christ, we can have the ability to surrender our sin to Him, rendering it ineffective in our lives. Sin no longer rules us for we now have a powerful weapon to keep it at bay.

D.L Moody said that, "The law tells me how crooked I am; Grace comes along and straightens me out." Before Jesus became our Savior, we were powerless to this "crookedness" in our lives. But now, through God's grace, He gives us what we need to resist temptation when we surrender that sin to Him.

When Jesus died, our old self died with Him. Likewise, our new self can now be offered as "instruments of righteousness." (v13) It is through Christ's death that we have the hope of being used by God for His purposes instead of being used by sin for selfish gratification.

Allow God's grace to work in your life by surrendering to Jesus the parts which are susceptible to destructive sin, and you can instead offer these parts as instruments of righteousness.

Where does the power lie in your life?
In sin ... or in God's grace?

When do you place more of an emphasis on sin in your life than on the grace of God that gives you the power to overcome?

How do you see yourself as a victim of sin instead of as a willing participant?

Heavenly Father,

There are no two ways around it; I am a hopeless sinner apart from Your saving grace offered through Your Son, Jesus Christ. Thank You for the opportunity You have given me to offer up what used to be only good for sin as an instrument of righteousness. This is nothing short of a miracle.

In Jesus' Name I pray,

Amen

Fifty Two Days of Grace

Now or Later?

"What then? Shall we sin because we are not under the law but under grace? By no means! Don't you know that when you offer yourselves to someone as obedient slaves, you are slaves of the one you obey — whether you are slaves to sin, which leads to death, or to obedience, which leads to righteousness? But thanks be to God that, though you used to be slaves to sin, you have come to obey from your heart the pattern of teaching that has now claimed your allegiance. You have been set free from sin and have become slaves to righteousness.

" I am using an example from everyday life because of your human limitations. Just as you used to offer yourselves as slaves to impurity and to ever-increasing wickedness, so now offer yourselves as slaves to righteousness leading to holiness. When you were slaves to sin, you were free from the control of righteousness. What benefit did you reap at that time from the things you are now ashamed of? Those things result in death! But now that you have been set free from sin and have become slaves of God, the benefit you reap leads to holiness, and the result is eternal life. For the wages of sin is death, but the gift of God is eternal life in Christ Jesus our Lord." (Romans 6:15-23)

Standing in line at the supermarket, it is hard to miss the headlines on the tabloids proclaiming one misdeed after another. I often wonder how those who live such a privileged life can get into such a mess. It really is no mystery, though, as Paul reveals in this passage.

Many believe that in order to live life to the fullest, you must be free from any restrictions, free from rules. "Live it up, for life is short," says the world. But Paul asks how this kind of thinking and lifestyle benefits us. What are the rewards of a life focused on self-gratification? In our human rationale, we think that focusing on accomplishing everything on our bucket-list will bring fulfillment. After all, we are doing exactly what we want to do! In the words of Frank Sinatra, "I did it my way!"

But under closer scrutiny, those who do it their way are never content and peaceful. Maybe French poet C.F. Ramuz said it best, "Man never has what he wants, because what he wants is everything." This is the crux of Paul's argument. Following our fleshly desires reaps no reward. We have nothing to show for all of our effort; nothing but heartache. The payoff in becoming slaves to God through faith in Jesus Christ, however, is holiness, and the result is eternal life. This kind of delayed gratification may be a hard sell in today's fast food economy, but for those who are looking toward eternity, life is a much better outcome than death.

Fifty Two Days of Grace

Author and inspirational speaker Brian Tracy believes, "The ability to discipline yourself to delay gratification in the short term in order to enjoy greater rewards in the long term is the indispensable pre-requisite for success." To be successful at following Christ, we must deny our immediate desires in order to seek God's desires, thus earning us rewards in heaven. This is delayed gratification at its best!

Seek satisfaction now and it will fade, Follow Christ instead, and in eternity you'll be paid.

How is your desire to please yourself the guide that determines your choices?

When is it most hard for you to delay self-gratification?

Heavenly Father,

Thank You for the free gift of salvation that comes through faith in Jesus Christ. Even though I know my salvation is secure, it is my longing to please You in the choices that I make. Therefore, I ask Your help in preferring Your desires above my own.
In Jesus' Name I pray,
Amen

Fifty Two Days of Grace

Till Death Do Us Part

"Do you not know, brothers and sisters—for I am speaking to those who know the law—that the law has authority over someone only as long as that person lives? For example, by law a married woman is bound to her husband as long as he is alive, but if her husband dies, she is released from the law that binds her to him. So then, if she has sexual relations with another man while her husband is still alive, she is called an adulteress. But if her husband dies, she is released from that law and is not an adulteress if she marries another man.

"So, my brothers and sisters, you also died to the law through the body of Christ, that you might belong to another, to him who was raised from the dead, in order that we might bear fruit for God. For when we were in the realm of the flesh, the sinful passions aroused by the law were at work in us, so that we bore fruit for death. But now, by dying to what once bound us, we have been released from the law so that we serve in the new way of the Spirit, and not in the old way of the written code. (Romans 7:1-6)

I always cry at weddings. I have even been to the wedding of one of my husband's coworkers whom I barely knew, and my eyes welled up during the vows. I think it is the gravity of the situation; the promise the couple is making before God and man to stay together, "'till death do us part."

When God created Eve, He made her from Adam so she would be a helpmate to him and so they would become one flesh upon marriage. This union is broken at the death of one or both spouses. Paul says, in the same way, our tie with the law is also broken by the death of Christ. We are no longer "married" to the law, and therefore are not obligated to be faithful to it. Instead, we are freed to be "married" to Christ and follow Him. In turn, the fruit of the Spirit will be borne in us.

In this new union, we are free to simply follow the leading of the Spirit, without the fear of breaking a law and receiving death. We have the assurance through the sacrifice of Christ that our sin is covered, freeing us from the heavy yoke of obedience to the law. Instead, we take up the yoke of Christ which "is easy and [His] burden is light." (Matthew 11:30) Following the law to the letter is a heavy burden and difficult task, one we can't do on our own. But God's Spirit, instead, enables us to learn from Jesus and follow Him one step at a time, a much less daunting assignment.

*Follow Jesus and be free from
the burden of the law.*

How do you live as if you were still bound to the Law?

Fifty Two Days of Grace

When do you try to earn salvation by placing a heavy burden upon yourself to live a godly, upright life?

Heavenly Father,

Thank You for setting me free from the law of sin and death. Through faith in Jesus Christ, I am now free to live a life in tandem with You. As I walk in step with Your Spirit, I will discover new fruit forming in my heart; fruit that is from You and pleasing to You.
In Jesus' Name I pray,
Amen

Fifty Two Days of Grace

Surrender our Minds

"So I find this law at work: Although I want to do good, evil is right there with me. For in my inner being I delight in God's law; but I see another law at work in me, waging war against the law of my mind and making me a prisoner of the law of sin at work within me. What a wretched man I am! Who will rescue me from this body that is subject to death? Thanks be to God, who delivers me through Jesus Christ our Lord!

"So then, I myself in my mind am a slave to God's law, but in my sinful nature, a slave to the law of sin.

"Therefore, there is now no condemnation for those who are in Christ Jesus, because through Christ Jesus the law of the Spirit who gives life has set you free from the law of sin and death. For what the law was powerless to do because it was weakened by the flesh, God did by sending his own Son in the likeness of sinful flesh to be a sin offering. And so he condemned sin in the flesh, in order that the righteous requirement of the law might be fully met in us, who do not live according to the flesh but according to the Spirit.

"Those who live according to the flesh have their minds set on what the flesh desires; but those who live in accordance with the Spirit have their minds set on what the Spirit desires. The mind governed by the flesh is death, but the mind governed by the Spirit is life and peace. The mind governed by the flesh is hostile to God; it does not submit to God's law, nor can it do so. Those who are in the realm of the flesh cannot please God.

"You, however, are not in the realm of the flesh but are in the realm of the Spirit, if indeed the Spirit of God lives in you. And if anyone does not have the Spirit of Christ, they do not belong to Christ. But if Christ is in you, then even though your body is subject to death because of sin, the Spirit gives life because of righteousness. And if the Spirit of him who raised Jesus from the dead is living in you, he who raised Christ from the dead will also give life to your mortal bodies because of his Spirit who lives in you."
(Romans 7:21-8:11)

"A mind is a terrible thing to waste," is the slogan of the United Negro College Fund. It has inspired many since 1972 to use the mind God gave them to better their lives. It implies that the power to change our circumstances lies within our mind. It has been a very successful campaign, and continues to be, but it is not a precept upon which we should base our lives.

In this passage, Paul clearly lays out the problem with allowing our minds to lead us. We may have every desire to follow God's law, in fact we may delight in it. But the sin living within us is constantly fighting against our desire to do good, and instead we end up doing the very evil we do not want to do. Sound like a familiar struggle? It is because we cannot, in our own strength, win the battle of our minds. Our mind sets us up for failure by tipping off the flesh, by betraying our innermost desire to follow God. Once our intentions are made known, sin gets to work fighting against anything righteous our minds focus on. What is our recourse? "Who will rescue (us) from this body of death?" (7:24-25) Not our willpower. Not our effort. Not diligent Bible study. Not regular church attendance. Our rescuer is Jesus Christ our Lord!

Jesus provides a new way to go about this battle of the flesh. Instead of letting our mind do the leading which results in being controlled by the flesh, we submit to God's Spirit, and thus are controlled by His Spirit. My mind makes my flesh rise up, making it impossible to please God (v8), while a mind surrendered to the Lord is a mind of life and peace. (v6)

> *"All to Jesus I surrender;*
> *Lord, I give myself to thee;*
> *fill me with thy love and power;*
> *let thy blessing fall on me.*
>
> *I surrender all, I surrender all,*
> *all to thee, my blessed Savior,*
> *I surrender all."**

Fifty Two Days of Grace

My mind is powerless against the flesh, which leads to death.

God's Spirit can lead my mind to life and peace.

When are you most vulnerable to the leading of your mind?

Which areas of your life do you most need to surrender to Jesus today?

Heavenly Father,
Thank You for the ability You give me through Your Spirit to overcome the power of sin in my life. Help me to resist the temptation to use will power or positive thoughts to fight the battle of sin, and instead submit to my Lord and Savior, Jesus Christ. Letting You lead will result in a life that pleases You.
In Jesus' Name I pray,
Amen

*"I Surrender All" **Text:** *J.W. Van Deventer* **Music:** *W.S. Weeden*

Different Strokes

"Therefore, brothers and sisters, we have an obligation — but it is not to the flesh, to live according to it. For if you live according to the flesh, you will die; but if by the Spirit you put to death the misdeeds of the body, you will live.

"For those who are led by the Spirit of God are the children of God. The Spirit you received does not make you slaves, so that you live in fear again; rather, the Spirit you received brought about your adoption to sonship. And by him we cry, 'Abba, Father.' The Spirit himself testifies with our spirit that we are God's children. Now if we are children, then we are heirs — heirs of God and co-heirs with Christ, if indeed we share in his sufferings in order that we may also share in his glory.

"I consider that our present sufferings are not worth comparing with the glory that will be revealed in us." (Romans 8:12-18)

I remember watching *Different Strokes* when I was a child, a sitcom about two brothers who were adopted by a wealthy widower. It was always fun to watch how the boys learned to fit into their new position as sons of privilege. They often forgot their new place and still thought of themselves as poor orphan boys, unable to fathom that their father held them in the same standing as his natural-born daughter. Eventually, they began to accept their new status and all the advantages and responsibilities that came with it.

It makes me think of our position as adopted sons and daughters of God. We are co-heirs with Christ, the Son of God. We share in His sufferings, but also in His glory (v 17). Do we realize how incredible that is? Despite our filth, our sin and our unrighteousness, we can become sons and daughters right along with Christ by committing our lives to Him. This position, however, carries with it a responsibility. We are obligated to be led by the Spirit of God, not by the sinful nature (v12-14). As heirs to Christ's glory, we must remember our position. We also must remember Who our Daddy is. Just like a rich young girl who has not a care in the world because she knows her daddy will take care of her and protect her, so should we be with our "Abba Father." It may be hard to trust anyone; we are all tainted by our experiences of being let down by those we love, but God is different. He keeps His promises. He can always be counted on to do what is best for us (whether we like it or not) and He will never leave us.

As adopted sons and daughters, we will share in Christ's glory. Paul wrote in his second letter to the Corinthians, chapter 4 verse 17, "For our light and momentary troubles are achieving for us an eternal glory that far outweighs them all." While we are here in this troubled world, we should live like we know who our Daddy is; secure in our position as sons and daughters of the Creator of the Universe, knowing that our suffering here is temporary and will lead to future glory.

> *As sons and daughters of the Creator, we*
> *can rest securely in His capable hands.*

When do I live my life as if I really don't matter, or as if my life holds no value?

How can I live more like the child of the King?

Heavenly Father,

It is remarkable to me that You love me enough to call me Your child. I'm thankful for the forgiveness You so freely extend through Christ. It is not easy for me to see myself as You do, but when I take on this new perspective, I understand how treasured my life is. Help me to live as Your treasured possession.
In Jesus' Name I pray,
Amen

Fifty Two Days of Grace

Master Plan

"In the same way, the Spirit helps us in our weakness. We do not know what we ought to pray for, but the Spirit himself intercedes for us through wordless groans. And he who searches our hearts knows the mind of the Spirit, because the Spirit intercedes for God's people in accordance with the will of God."
(Romans 8:26-27)

John Bunyan, author of the beloved *Pilgrim's Progress* believed that, "In prayer it is better to have a heart without words than words without heart." There are many times I pray without thinking, repeating words I have said a million times by rote. My heart is not really a part of this kind of praying. But the times when my heart aches and I have no words to pray are the times when I truly experience a connection with my Father. The Spirit takes over and prays for what God wants. It is during these prayers when the words just flow from this unseen source that I learn God's will. On my own, I have no idea how to pray when a woman commits suicide, or my daughter is defiant, or when I just feel depressed. When I open my heart to my Father, His Spirit goes to work praying on my behalf, thus revealing His will for the situation.

The difference between praying our will and God's will is highlighted in the words of Arthur W. Pink, an early 20th century Evangelist and Bible scholar. "The prevailing idea seems to be, that I come to God and ask Him for something I want, and that I expect Him to give me that which I have asked. But this is a most dishonouring and degrading conception. The popular belief reduces God to a servant, our servant: doing our bidding, performing our pleasure, granting our desires. No, prayer is a coming to God, telling Him my need, committing my way unto the Lord, and leaving Him to deal with it as seemeth Him best." Prayer is not about requesting what we want or think we need or performing some kind of heartless ritual, but is an act of surrendering our will in exchange for His. It is about crying out to Him and letting Him work out the details according to His plan.

When I was younger, I often wondered why many Christians sounded the same when they prayed. I thought, in my ignorance, that perhaps they all took a class on how to pray, learning the lingo and proper techniques. But as I've grown in my walk and have witnessed God's Spirit taking over a prayer, I understand. It was not the believers I had heard praying, but God's Spirit.

Prayer is a window to God's will and an opportunity to surrender to the Master Planner.

How often do you use prayer as a magic talisman to manipulate circumstances to your liking?

Fifty Two Days of Grace

When do you pray for specific outcomes instead of letting God decide what's best for you?

Heavenly Father,

I have to admit that I like to be in control of my own life. In order to follow You, however, I must submit myself to You and let You lead. I give this day to You, then, Father, and ask that Your will be done. Help me to stay out of the way of Your master plan and instead simply submit.
In Jesus' Name I pray,
Amen

Fifty Two Days of Grace

The Good Pain

"And we know that in all things God works for the good of those who love him, who have been called according to his purpose." (Romans 8:28)

"Woosh, smack, woosh, smack!" The sound of the paddle hitting my back side resonated in the air.

"This is for your own good," my dad said as he finished the job. *What possible good could this bring?* my seven-year-old mind thought as my behind stung from the blows inflicted by my father. At the time, I did not understand how this spanking could have been good in any way, but my father knew that it was necessary for my character development. In his wisdom, he understood that his child needed to learn the consequences for her actions. Ouch!

Our Father in heaven is also devoted to our character development. He uses whatever means He deems necessary to transform us into the likeness of Jesus. God has a way of taking what we label as the worst thing that ever happened to us, and revealing it as the most pivotal moment in our lives, responsible for bringing about more good than anything else ever had.

As mere humans, we don't always see the good that comes out of the difficult. This is usually something God shows us over time. But God is always in control, working to refine us, guide us and mold us. Olympic athlete and missionary Eric

Liddell said, "Circumstances may appear to wreck our lives and God's plans, but God is not helpless among the ruins. Our broken lives are not lost or useless. God comes in and takes calamity and uses it victoriously, working out his wonderful plan of love."

What we perceive as pain, God means for good.

When do you fight against the hard things in life, forgetting that God is using them for good?

How can you refocus your attention on God and His good plan during times of trial?

Heavenly Father,
Thank You for loving me enough to discipline me, using the difficulties and hardships to transform me into the person You've created me to be. As I go through these painful times, help me to remember the good You've promised as a result.
In Jesus' Name I pray,
Amen

More than Conquerors

"For those God foreknew he also predestined to be conformed to the image of his Son, that he might be the firstborn among many brothers and sisters. And those he predestined, he also called; those he called, he also justified; those he justified, he also glorified.

"What, then, shall we say in response to these things? If God is for us, who can be against us? He who did not spare his own Son, but gave him up for us all — how will he not also, along with him, graciously give us all things? Who will bring any charge against those whom God has chosen? It is God who justifies. Who then is the one who condemns? No one. Christ Jesus who died — more than that, who was raised to life — is at the right hand of God and is also interceding for us. Who shall separate us from the love of Christ? Shall trouble or hardship or persecution or famine or nakedness or danger or sword? As it is written:

"'For your sake we face death all day long; we are considered as sheep to be slaughtered.'

No, in all these things we are more than conquerors through him who loved us. For I am convinced that neither death nor life, neither angels nor demons, neither the present nor the future, nor any powers, neither height nor depth, nor anything else in all creation, will be able to

separate us from the love of God that is in Christ Jesus our Lord." (Romans 8: 29-39)

Have you ever felt like the whole world is out to get you? "No good deed goes unpunished," seems to be the precept upon which humanity is based. My husband recently retired from 24 years of active duty in the Army. Throughout those years, he was accused of doing things he would never think of doing: molesting a subordinate's wife, ogling women soldiers as they showered, neglecting his duties. In reality, he cared about his soldiers and tried to do the best job possible in serving his country. Sometimes, though, he felt that everyone was out to get him.

The truth, however, tells a different story. "If God is for us, who can be against us?" This passage tells us that God knows us, chose us, called us, justified us and glorified us. What accuser, human or spirit, can overcome all that God has put in our corner? Therefore, we can stand in calm assurance that He will prevail. People can try, but they won't succeed in bringing about circumstances that are outside of God's will: It just can't happen.

Abraham Lincoln understood this principle. He believed, ". . . the will of God prevails; without him all human reliance is vain; without the assistance of that Divine Being I cannot succeed; with that assistance I cannot fail." Unfounded accusations used to try to bring you down will not succeed, unless God purposes to use it for the good.

Fifty Two Days of Grace

Nothing can stand against the power of God.
On His side, we are more than conquerors!

When do you panic as things seem to be spiraling out of control, as if God has left His post?

How do you live as a victim instead of a conqueror?

Heavenly Father,
Thank You for Your love that enables me to stand firm against any foe. When I'm feeling under attack or as if I have no hope, help me to remember the power that comes from staying close to You. If You are for me, there is no one that can stand against the plan You have for my life. In this promise I will trust.
In Jesus' Name I pray,
Amen

Fifty Two Days of Grace

Father Abraham

"I speak the truth in Christ — I am not lying, my conscience confirms it through the Holy Spirit — I have great sorrow and unceasing anguish in my heart. For I could wish that I myself were cursed and cut off from Christ for the sake of my people, those of my own race, the people of Israel. Theirs is the adoption to sonship; theirs the divine glory, the covenants, the receiving of the law, the temple worship and the promises. Theirs are the patriarchs, and from them is traced the human ancestry of the Messiah, who is God over all, forever praised! Amen.

"It is not as though God's word had failed. For not all who are descended from Israel are Israel. Nor because they are his descendants are they all Abraham's children. On the contrary, 'It is through Isaac that your offspring will be reckoned.' In other words, it is not the children by physical descent who are God's children, but it is the children of the promise who are regarded as Abraham's offspring. For this was how the promise was stated: 'At the appointed time I will return, and Sarah will have a son.'"
(Romans 9:1-9)

"Father Abraham, had many sons, and many sons had father Abraham. I am one of them, and so are you, so let's just praise the Lord!" Do you remember this children's Sunday school song? Fun as it is to sing, it also imparts a great truth. We now are a part of the nation of Israel, of God's chosen people, of the line of David. Tradition, blood line and ancestry no longer hold any weight. Under the new covenant, we can enjoy the blessings and promises given to Abraham through faith in Jesus Christ.

India has long used a caste system in which people are born into one of five different levels. Once born into a certain category, there is no changing; this is the position in which one will marry, give birth and die. There is no opportunity for anyone to move up or down a caste. Thankfully, this is not the case with God's Kingdom. He has provided a way that anyone, from any walk of life or culture, can join His family simply by accepting His free gift of salvation through Jesus Christ our Lord. It is then that we can join with all the saints, past and present, in being considered as a descendent of Abraham.

What a privilege to know the Creator as our Father,
and to be welcomed freely into His family.

When do you live as if you must earn the right to be called a child of God?

How can you honor your adopted heavenly Father in the way you live your life?

Heavenly Father,

What love You have lavished upon me that I am called Your child! I can barely fathom such a thought, yet this is what You have done for me in sending Your precious Son to die a criminal's death. Help me to live as one who is part of Your eternal family, valuing each moment as priceless.

In Jesus' Name I pray,

Amen

Fifty Two Days of Grace

Comfortable Shoes

"It does not, therefore, depend on human desire or effort, but on God's mercy. For Scripture says to Pharaoh: 'I raised you up for this very purpose, that I might display my power in you and that my name might be proclaimed in all the earth.' Therefore God has mercy on whom he wants to have mercy, and he hardens whom he wants to harden.

"One of you will say to me: 'Then why does God still blame us? For who is able to resist his will?' But who are you, a human being, to talk back to God? 'Shall what is formed say to the one who formed it, "Why did you make me like this"?' Does not the potter have the right to make out of the same lump of clay some pottery for special purposes and some for common use?

"What if God, although choosing to show his wrath and make his power known, bore with great patience the objects of his wrath — prepared for destruction? What if he did this to make the riches of his glory known to the objects of his mercy, whom he prepared in advance for glory — even us, whom he also called, not only from the Jews but also from the Gentiles?"
(Romans 9:16-24)

I sometimes contract a severe case of compare-itis, judging my perception of myself to my view of others. I have suffered long from this condition, as evidenced by the advice my mother gave me as a teen fretting about the perfection of the other girls in my class. "Don't worry," she said, "they have plenty of problems, too." It was comforting to think about, but all I could see was their beautifully clear skin, their attractive personality, and their angelic voice singing for the admiration of all who heard. Why couldn't I have some of those qualities?

It reminds me of a quote I read from an 18th-century Hassidic master, Rabbi Zusya. He said, "In the world to come, I shall not be asked, 'Why were you not Moses?' I shall be asked, 'Why were you not Zusya?'" It is easy to fall into the trap of trying to become what we think we should be (or what we think others expect us to be), instead of fully blossoming into the men and woman God created us to be. Each of us has been given some awesome gifts to use to further His kingdom. To discover these, embrace them, and use them must give our Father much pleasure. God has also created each of us with a unique make-up; a way of looking at the world that is distinct. When we acknowledge this and use it to His advantage, there is no job God can't use us to accomplish!

Revering and honoring our Creator means we must accept the way He "knit us together". (Psalm 139:13) Comparing ourselves to others only serves to dishonor God, and tear us down. But embracing the pottery He is fashioning out of the lowly lump of clay that is us, serves to honor God to the highest degree. It is not about self-esteem, but God-esteem. By accepting ourselves, we are telling God we trust His plan for our lives.

Stepping into our shoes and feeling comfortable means being ready to travel wherever God calls us to go!

How do you strive to be someone else other than who God made you to be?

When are you focusing more on your own plan for your life than on God's?

Heavenly Father,

Thank You for creating a specific, unique plan for my life, and for fashioning me in just the way You desired. Help me to accept myself in the way You have designed me and may I flourish wherever You place me. I praise you because I am fearfully and wonderfully made!

In Jesus' Name I pray,
Amen

Fifty Two Days of Grace

Stumbling Stone

"As he says in Hosea: 'I will call them "my people" who are not my people; and I will call her "my loved one" who is not my loved one,' and, 'In the very place where it was said to them, "You are not my people," there they will be called "children of the living God."'

Isaiah cries out concerning Israel: 'Though the number of the Israelites be like the sand by the sea, only the remnant will be saved. For the Lord will carry out his sentence on earth with speed and finality.'

It is just as Isaiah said previously: 'Unless the Lord Almighty had left us descendants, we would have become like Sodom, we would have been like Gomorrah.'

What then shall we say? That the Gentiles, who did not pursue righteousness, have obtained it, a righteousness that is by faith; but the people of Israel, who pursued the law as the way of righteousness, have not attained their goal. Why not? Because they pursued it not by faith but as if it were by works. They stumbled over the stumbling stone. As it is written: 'See, I lay in Zion a stone that causes people to stumble and a rock that makes them fall, and the one who believes in him will never be put to shame.'"
(Romans 9:25-33)

A woman in our church told me the story of her family's heritage of faith which reached back to a time before the reformation. She went on to describe how her ancestors left the faith and that she, in the 20th Century, was somehow returned to her descendant's legacy through faith in Jesus Christ. She couldn't understand why she, out of all of her family, (her unbelieving parents, aunts, uncles, siblings and cousins) was plucked from the fire. She is committed to praying for the rest of her family, pleading God to change their hearts and draw them to Jesus. (John 6:65)

What a sobering illustration of the path of salvation. None of us comes to the foot of the cross on our own steam. Under the old covenant given to Abraham, Isaac and Jacob, God's people were required to do (and not do) many things. These actions and lifestyle were, in part, what set them apart from the rest of the world. Their hair was different, their eating practices peculiar, their rituals of sacrifice seemed strange. By doing as God had commanded, they were showing themselves to be God's chosen people. God, however, was always the One who chose His people and it was this designation that truly set them apart.

Under the new covenant, we are saved by a simple faith in Jesus. Through this grace we receive the Holy Spirit which, in turn, produces fruit which sets us apart from the rest of the world. But this grace is a stumbling stone because it takes us fully out of the picture and places Jesus solely in the center. We play no part in our salvation. Our family heritage plays no part in our salvation. Our ability to make a wise decision plays no part in our salvation. To God's glory alone, we as believers are labeled as His chosen people. (v 25-26)

The work God does in our hearts is what gives us the faith to repent and be saved. Preacher and Civil War Chaplain Thomas Brooks illustrates this truth well. "Saving grace makes a man as willing to leave his lusts as a slave is willing to leave his galley, or a prisoner his dungeon, or a thief his bolts, or a beggar his rags."

God inclines our hearts toward Jesus,
shines a spotlight on the narrow gate of salvation
and propels us through to glory.

Why is it important that you understand that you played no part in your own salvation?

When is it most hard to believe that you cannot save yourself?

Heavenly Father,
Thank You for the gift of salvation that comes through faith in Jesus Christ. Without this unspeakable gift, I would be destined to live a life devoid of hope, peace and love. Help me to keep my true identity as a sinner saved by grace always at the forefront of my mind. In Jesus' Name I pray,
Amen

Fifty Two Days of Grace

Your Way, or God's Way?

"Brothers and sisters, my heart's desire and prayer to God for the Israelites is that they may be saved. For I can testify about them that they are zealous for God, but their zeal is not based on knowledge. Since they did not know the righteousness of God and sought to establish their own, they did not submit to God's righteousness. Christ is the culmination of the law so that there may be righteousness for everyone who believes.

"Moses writes this about the righteousness that is by the law: 'The person who does these things will live by them.'" (Romans 10:1-5)

I can remember receiving visits from a certain cult, of sorts, from the time I was a young child. The way we handled these visits in my parent's home was to hide. "Quick! They're coming to the door! Hide in the kitchen and be still until they are gone!" As a teenager, I remember being caught in the driveway while washing the car when this persistent group drove up. I had no choice but to greet them. As a young believer, I sensed their message was off, but couldn't put my finger on what was wrong. As I grew up and established a home of my own, these zealous people continued to visit, no matter in which state or country we lived. Their persistence and zeal always struck me. I wondered how they could be so darned determined to give their message despite the unwelcoming behavior they no doubt received on a regular basis. What propelled them to continue their mission when I knew in my heart that it was not from God? Reading this passage draws my mind to this religious sect. They are extremely enthusiastic about God, but their zeal is not based on Truth. They have taken what they have read and, using their own minds, have interpreted the message in a way that is contrary to God's intended purpose. In attempting to create their own way of becoming right with God, they have rejected the divinity of Christ as well as the message of grace which comes through the cross.

Paul is clear in this passage that our righteousness does not come from doing things our way, but God's way. And His way allows for salvation only for those who believe that Jesus is the only way. If we try another way, like following the law, we are bound to it. We must follow every law without fail. Impossible! The entire purpose of Jesus sacrificing himself on the cross was so that we could be saved from the futility of "righteousness by the law." (v 5) Which brings me back to the Witnesses: they have been convinced that in order for them to be saved, they must fulfill certain rules established by man. If not, they believe they are doomed to eternal damnation. How sad when the Truth can be found in the pages of the very book they carry in their hands each time they knock on a door.

Fifty Two Days of Grace

Let no man distract you from the
Truth: Jesus is the Only Way!

When do you most struggle with doing things your way
instead of God's?

How is it difficult to believe the truth of the Gospel?

Heavenly Father,
It is my desire to be zealous for the Truth of the
Gospel, reaching out to others to shed light upon the path
of salvation that comes only through Christ. Help me to
stay true to Your way and to let go of my desire to try to
earn salvation. I know that Jesus is the only way to You,
Father.
In Jesus' Name I pray,
Amen

Fifty Two Days of Grace

Blind-sided

"If some of the branches have been broken off,
and you, though a wild olive shoot, have been
grafted in among the others and now share in the
nourishing sap from the olive root, do not
consider yourself to be superior to those other
branches. If you do, consider this: You do not
support the root, but the root supports you. You
will say then, 'Branches were broken off so that I
could be grafted in.' Granted. But they were
broken off because of unbelief, and you stand by
faith. Do not be arrogant, but tremble. For if God
did not spare the natural branches, he will not
spare you either.

"Consider therefore the kindness and
sternness of God: sternness to those who fell, but
kindness to you, provided that you continue in his
kindness. Otherwise, you also will be cut off.
And if they do not persist in unbelief, they will be
grafted in, for God is able to graft them in again.
After all, if you were cut out of an olive tree that is
wild by nature, and contrary to nature were
grafted into a cultivated olive tree, how much
more readily will these, the natural branches, be
grafted into their own olive tree!"
(Romans 11:17-24)

"Resting on my laurels." This phrase brings to
mind an athlete who has always been at the top of
his game until one day, some young competitor

sweeps up and takes his place. The veteran never knew what hit him as he no longer stands at the pinnacle of his sport. His mistake was that he began to believe his own press and think he was invincible, ceasing the striving for perfection which got him to the high-point in which he had been enjoying. This arrogance allowed the above mentioned blind-side all too easy to pull off.

The same thing can happen to us as believers. We are brought into God's family as orphans, saved by faith through the mercy and grace of God and the sacrifice of His Son. Once we get over the initial excitement of this miracle of salvation, it is easy to fall into a lackadaisical state, forgetting the example of Paul in Philippians 3:14. "I strain to reach the end of the race and receive the prize for which God, through Christ Jesus, is calling us up to heaven." (NLT) Instead, it is too easy to stop reaching toward the finish line and become content to stay where we are: Content with our salvation and place in God's kingdom. The problem is, when we are not moving forward, as my Sunday school teacher says, we are in reality moving backward.

Let us not become content with the miracle of being grafted onto the cultivated olive tree (v 24), but rejoice in our ability to grow closer to our Father with each passing day. As writer and editor Robert Turtle said, "The Christian walk is much like riding a bicycle; we are either moving forward or falling off."

Do you ever feel like you are stuck in a rut when it comes to your relationship with the Lord?

How can you guard against complacency?

Heavenly Father,
Thank You for this indescribable gift of salvation. I often take it for granted, losing sight of the unspeakable sacrifice Jesus made on my behalf. Help me not to grow complacent, but to strive every moment toward my heavenly goal.
In Jesus' Name I pray,
Amen

Fifty Two Days of Grace

Written on Our Hearts

"I do not want you to be ignorant of this mystery, brothers and sisters, so that you may not be conceited: Israel has experienced a hardening in part until the full number of the Gentiles has come in, and in this way all Israel will be saved. As it is written: 'The deliverer will come from Zion; he will turn godlessness away from Jacob. And this is my covenant with them when I take away their sins.'

"As far as the gospel is concerned, they are enemies for your sake; but as far as election is concerned, they are loved on account of the patriarchs, for God's gifts and his call are irrevocable. Just as you who were at one time disobedient to God have now received mercy as a result of their disobedience, so they too have now become disobedient in order that they too may now receive mercy as a result of God's mercy to you.

"For God has bound everyone over to disobedience so that he may have mercy on them all. Oh, the depth of the riches of the wisdom and knowledge of God! How unsearchable his judgments and his paths beyond tracing out! 'Who has known the mind of the Lord? Or who has been his counselor? 'Who has ever given to God, that God should repay them?' For from him and through him and for him are all things to him be the glory forever! Amen." (Romans 11:25-36)

There is a prophecy tied to this passage which tells of God's plan to forgive the wickedness of His people and remember their sins no more. (Jeremiah 31:31-34) According to this passage, it is a part of a covenant the Lord made with the house of Israel that He would put His laws in our minds and write them on our hearts so that we each would be held accountable for our own actions. In this way, each of us has the opportunity to be forgiven when we repent of our sins and turn to the Lord Jesus as our Savior.

The great 19th Century preacher, Charles Spurgeon, taught about this mystery of God's law being written on our heart. He said, "A man with whom God the Holy Spirit deals is one who does not have to go to the 20th of Exodus to know what the law is; he does not need to stop and ask concerning most things, 'Is this right?' or, 'Is this wrong?' but he carries within him a balance and a scale, a standard and test by which he can try these things for himself. He has the law of his God written upon his heart, so that, almost as soon as he looks at a thing, he begins to perceive whether there is evil in it or whether it is good. There is a sort of sensitiveness in his soul which makes him discern between good and evil." It is this discernment from God which can either be followed, or ignored. When we do things our way, we are making a conscious decision to act contrary to what God has written on our hearts. We really have no excuse. We cannot say, "I didn't know. . .no one ever told me." We would be better off taking on the motto of the British Foreign Service. "Never excuse. Never explain. Never complain." Phew, that's a lot of pressure!

Thankfully, we are not without hope. The same Spirit that makes us aware of God's law, also enables us to delight in it and to desire to do things God's way. We can find this back in Romans seven when Paul said his heart delights in God's law, but he needed Jesus Christ in order to follow it instead of the law of his sinful nature. Through faith in Jesus, the indwelling Spirit of God empowers us to not only love God's ways, but to follow Him as well.

With God's law written on our heart, we are without excuse. But we are not without hope!

When do I easily excuse my sinful ways?

How can the hope I have in Christ spur me on to follow His Spirit instead of my own lustful ways?

Heavenly Father,
You have given me the benefit of Your indwelling Spirit to show me the way You would have me to go. Often, though, I choose my own way instead. Help me to prefer Your ways over mine and remind me of the power You have given me to choose such a path. In Jesus' Name I pray,
Amen

Fifty Two Days of Grace

Our God: Promise Keeper

"I do not want you to be ignorant of this mystery, brothers and sisters, so that you may not be conceited: Israel has experienced a hardening in part until the full number of the Gentiles has come in, and in this way all Israel will be saved. As it is written:

'The deliverer will come from Zion; he will turn godlessness away from Jacob. And this is my covenant with them when I take away their sins.'

As far as the gospel is concerned, they are enemies for your sake; but as far as election is concerned, they are loved on account of the patriarchs, for God's gifts and his call are irrevocable. Just as you who were at one time disobedient to God have now received mercy as a result of their disobedience, so they too have now become disobedient in order that they too may now receive mercy as a result of God's mercy to you. For God has bound everyone over to disobedience so that he may have mercy on them all.

"Oh, the depth of the riches of the wisdom and knowledge of God! How unsearchable his judgments, and his paths beyond tracing out! 'Who has known the mind of the Lord? Or who has been his counselor?' 'Who has ever given to God, that God should repay them?' For from him and through him and for him are all things. To him be the glory forever! Amen."

(Romans 11:25-36)

How often do we study God's Word, read devotionals, or work through Bible studies only to be searching for how it applies to our own lives and how it can make us stronger followers of Christ? There is nothing wrong with this, but today's passage fills me with a desire to focus solely on the character of the God we worship.

The God of Abraham, Isaac and Jacob, the Creator of Heaven and Earth, is a God who keeps His promises. Nowhere is it more vividly illustrated than in this passage. Verses 28-29, "As far as the gospel is concerned, they (the Jews) are enemies on your account: but as far as election is concerned, they are loved on account of the patriarchs, for God's gifts and his call are irrevocable. "

Thousands of years ago God promised Abraham that he would be the father of many nations and that all people would be blessed through him. This promise has been fulfilled through the nation of Israel and the blood of Jesus. The Lord has gone even further by promising never to leave His chosen people. After anointing Saul King of Israel in I Samuel 12, he goes on to deliver a message from God in verse 22, "For the LORD will not forsake his people for his great name's sake: because it hath pleased the LORD to make you his people." This message is repeated over and over again as His chosen people go through king after king, many of them evil, and year after year of straying away from God's ways. Despite the behavior of His people, God loves them. He loves them because it pleases Him to have chosen them to be His people.

God does not give up on us, not because we are valuable in and of ourselves or are inherently good. We are only these things because He has chosen us and has given us His grace. The Lord stays with us because that is Who He Is. He told Moses, "I am Who I Am." The reputation of His Name throughout His creation allows no other scenario but to stick with those He has chosen.

Let's just meditate on this one aspect of God; He keeps His Word. As a result, we are able to have a relationship with our Father through faith in Jesus Christ because of who God is: He is a God who keeps His promises.

> *We never have to worry that our Father will leave us, His very makeup will not allow it!*

How does focusing on God and His character help you to trust Him?

When do you try to turn every scripture around to you and your life, only caring about how it applies to you?

Heavenly Father,
You are a God who keeps His promises. Due to this important part of Your character, I can always trust

You to do as You have said You will do. Help me to remember that You are not like a human, prone to changing Your mind or forgetting to follow through. Instead, You are incapable of failing.

In Jesus' Name I pray,

Amen

A Higher Purpose

"'May their eyes be darkened so they cannot see, and their backs be bent forever.'

"Again I ask: Did they stumble so as to fall beyond recovery? Not at all! Rather, because of their transgression, salvation has come to the Gentiles to make Israel envious. But if their transgression means riches for the world, and their loss means riches for the Gentiles, how much greater riches will their full inclusion bring!

"I am talking to you Gentiles. Inasmuch as I am the apostle to the Gentiles, I take pride in my ministry in the hope that I may somehow arouse my own people to envy and save some of them. For if their rejection brought reconciliation to the world, what will their acceptance be but life from the dead? If the part of the dough offered as firstfruits is holy, then the whole batch is holy; if the root is holy, so are the branches."
(Romans 11:10-16)

The mother of a friend of my daughter's is suffering from a mystery condition. Her family says she is not the same strong godly woman they have always known. Instead, she has withdrawn to a near catatonic state and sits idly in bed, day after day, seemingly oblivious to the world around her. Doctors can find no cause for her infirmity. This trial, however, has brought about a change in her family; her husband has stepped up to fill the role of the spiritual leader of their family of seven, a position previously held by his wife. The oldest daughter has realized her need to "work out her own salvation with fear and trembling" and has grown closer to Jesus. She talks about how her mother was always her spiritual rock, the one she could always count on to set her straight. Now, she is looking to Jesus to fill that role. This family's tragedy is being used by God to bring about "greater riches"; the kind of riches that can only be spent in heaven; the kind of riches this world does not recognize.

I believe this is the kind of thing Paul is referring to in today's passage. The disbelief of the Jews has been used purposefully to bring the gospel message to the rest of the world. And scripture says their loss is our gain. It sounds an awful lot like the Israelites, God's chosen people, are being sacrificed for our sake, so that we may become His chosen people through faith. I don't know about you, but this idea of sacrifice makes me uncomfortable. But it is this very concept on which our entire salvation rests: the sacrifice of the One perfect Jew to bring us righteousness and life everlasting.

It reminds me of a story I heard about a young man who was severely burned in a boiler explosion. Doctors used 6000 square centimeters of skin from a donor to save his life. The patient said he couldn't bear to think about the fact that he was alive because of a dead donor. It was a concept too big, too much, so he couldn't think about it: A sacrifice so tremendous that it touched him to his soul. Similarly, the Jews have unknowingly made a sacrifice. But we can be assured that their acceptance of the gospel will mean life from the dead just as it does for anyone else. (v 15-16) Let's thank God for the Jews, and pray for their salvation.

> *God's ways are upside down and*
> *backwards compared to our ways.*

When do you get caught up trying to understand the "why" of a situation?

How can you live in a way that honors the sacrifice that brought you new life?

Heavenly Father,
I praise You for being a God whose ways are so much higher than my own. Since Your thoughts are not the same as mine, I can't expect to understand the way Your mind works. Therefore, it is my intention that I trust You enough to leave my desire to comprehend Your purposes behind, and simply walk by faith.
In Jesus' Name I pray,
Amen

Fifty Two Days of Grace

True Worship

"Therefore, I urge you, brothers and sisters, in view of God's mercy, to offer your bodies as a living sacrifice, holy and pleasing to God—this is your true and proper worship. Do not conform to the pattern of this world, but be transformed by the renewing of your mind. Then you will be able to test and approve what God's will is—his good, pleasing and perfect will." (Romans 12: 1-2)

How do you worship? In this country, when we hear the word "worship", visions of musicians and singers leading us in songs of praise to God comes to mind. But this passage tells us that worship is much more than that. It is the constant act of offering our flesh, the very thing that can work to separate us from God, as a living sacrifice to Him. The secret to true worship of God is giving our own desires continually over to Him so that He can use us as He wills.

This means when I feel my irritation level rise when dealing with difficult people, I need to immediately go to God and give Him my pride and allow Him to love them through me. Or when the traffic is eating away my time and I feel my stress levels rise, I give Him my desire to control my own destiny and submit myself to the position my Father has placed me in at that moment, trusting Him with my time. Or when tension mounts in my home, I will drop my own selfish point-of-view and ask God for His, allowing me to see the hurt that lies beneath the harsh words. All of these scenarios are forms of worship of God. All of them result in God's work and thus glorification of His Name.

The world and our fleshly desires are constantly pulling us toward them, but a love of these things douses the richness and miracle of the closeness of God's Spirit within us. Let us instead invite God into every aspect of our lives, resulting in true worship that pleases Him.

Worship is more than singing, but a constant surrendering of our own desires.

How are you vulnerable to adopting the ways of the world?

When do you easily let your fleshly desires rule instead of submitting yourself to your heavenly Father?

Heavenly Father,

It is easy for me to think I can only worship You in a formal, corporate setting. Your Word, however, tells me that each moment I live provides an opportunity to give praise to You. Help me to constantly be aware of the worldly and fleshly influences on my life, and help me to choose You instead.

In Jesus' Name I pray,

Amen

Source of Light

"Love must be sincere. Hate what is evil; cling to what is good. Be devoted to one another in love. Honor one another above yourselves. Never be lacking in zeal, but keep your spiritual fervor, serving the Lord. Be joyful in hope, patient in affliction, faithful in prayer. Share with the Lord's people who are in need. Practice hospitality.

"Bless those who persecute you; bless and do not curse. Rejoice with those who rejoice; mourn with those who mourn. Live in harmony with one another. Do not be proud, but be willing to associate with people of low position. Do not be conceited.

"Do not repay anyone evil for evil. Be careful to do what is right in the eyes of everyone. If it is possible, as far as it depends on you, live at peace with everyone." (Romans 12:9-18)

Living in a community is hard. We have to constantly be aware of how our actions affect our neighbors. If I mow my lawn too early, I may wake up my sleeping neighbor. If my daughter plays her music too loudly, it may disrupt the peace of the cul-de-sac. If my neighbors shoot off fireworks in the street in front of my house, they not only drive my dogs crazy but endanger the safety of my family's life and property. As neighbors living in a congested community, we must be sensitive to the people living around us. We can't just do whatever we please.

This is similar to the way Paul is instructing us to live as a community of believers. There is a whole list of guidelines, but he sums it up in verses 17 and 18. "Be careful to do what is right in the eyes of everybody. If it is possible, as far as it depends on you, live at peace with everyone." One of my friends once told me she listens to secular music because God shows her the heart of the songwriter through the words he has written. One day while driving through the neighborhood with her windows down and the music blaring, she passed a fellow believer who scowled with disapproval at the thumping coming from her sister's car. She clearly found my friend's choice of music "unchristian-like." Unfortunately, she did not know of my friend's calling and assumed she was becoming like the rest of the world. I'm sure a lot of judging took place in that woman's heart, but that all could have been avoided if my friend had kept her music to herself.

Let's face it; we don't need any incentive to judge each other as a body of believers: It is far too easy. Therefore, we need to do everything we can to avoid bruising another's sensibilities, giving them a tempting opening to judge us. We must be careful to not cause a brother or sister to stumble. As Jean Vanier, founder of an international organization which brought people with disabilities and their caregivers together in community has said, "There are times when together we discover that we make up a single body, that we belong to each other, and that God has called us to be together as a source of life for each other."

Being aware of how our actions effects our family makes us conscious of our choices.

When do you make choices based on the belief that your life is your own to do with as you see fit?

How have you been led into sin by another believer's actions?

Heavenly Father,

You have placed me together in a community of other believers, designing us to live in tandem with You and each other. Therefore, it is important that I am sensitive to how my actions are perceived, placing the choice to protect family members above my desire to live autonomously. Since this way of living is foreign to my independent mindset, I need Your grace to be able to think and act in such a way.

In Jesus' Name I pray,

Amen

Fifty Two Days of Grace

Responsible Citizen

"Let everyone be subject to the governing authorities, for there is no authority except that which God has established. The authorities that exist have been established by God. Consequently, whoever rebels against the authority is rebelling against what God has instituted, and those who do so will bring judgment on themselves. For rulers hold no terror for those who do right, but for those who do wrong. Do you want to be free from fear of the one in authority? Then do what is right and you will be commended. For the one in authority is God's servant for your good. But if you do wrong, be afraid, for rulers do not bear the sword for no reason. They are God's servants, agents of wrath to bring punishment on the wrongdoer. Therefore, it is necessary to submit to the authorities, not only because of possible punishment but also as a matter of conscience.

"This is also why you pay taxes, for the authorities are God's servants, who give their full time to governing. Give to everyone what you owe them: If you owe taxes, pay taxes; if revenue, then revenue; if respect, then respect; if honor, then honor." (Romans 13:1-7)

Rebelling against authority is something we've all done at one time or another, whether it be against our parents, teachers, principals, bosses, political leaders, the IRS or even law enforcement. There is something in the human spirit which wants to do things our way. This is never more obvious than in the eyes of a two-year-old who does not want to eat. You can see the determination to hold out against his parent's direction to "eat." No amount of coaxing will get the stubborn toddler to give in. The strength of our will is amazing. It reminds me of a story I heard about a four-year old girl who learned one of the names of God is "I am that I Am." True to her contrary spirit, she strode around the house for days after watching the movie *The Ten Commandments* pronouncing, "I'm not that I'm not."

In looking closer at this passage, however, I can see how much trouble this spirit of rebellion makes in our hearts. When we rebel against any authority placed over us, we are rebelling against God who placed them in that position. Nothing happens outside the will of God. We are to submit ourselves to authority instituted by men for the Lord's sake. (I Peter 2:13-14) It is not to keep us out of trouble, although that is a nice side-effect, or to make us look especially good, but it is to reflect well on the God we claim to follow. When we refuse to pay taxes, we look just like the rest of the world. When we do the right thing despite our disagreement with it, we honor the God we worship. In turn, others take note and wonder *Who is this God that even His people obey rules made my men?*

Fifty Two Days of Grace

A responsible believer is a responsible citizen, to the glory of God!

When do you struggle with submitting to authority?

How do you stand firm "for the principle of the thing" instead of following rules or laws with which you don't agree?

Heavenly Father,
I live in a world filled with people who have authority over me. For the times when I struggle to obey, give me the grace to be able to see the witness I am giving to a lost world who is watching. Putting my testimony above my rights may bring You glory in ways I never before realized.
In Jesus' Name I pray,
Amen

Fifty Two Days of Grace

Armor of Light

"Let no debt remain outstanding, except the continuing debt to love one another, for whoever loves others has fulfilled the law. The commandments, 'You shall not commit adultery,' 'You shall not murder,' 'You shall not steal,' 'You shall not covet,' and whatever other command there may be, are summed up in this one command: 'Love your neighbor as yourself.' Love does no harm to a neighbor. Therefore love is the fulfillment of the law.

"And do this, understanding the present time: The hour has already come for you to wake up from your slumber, because our salvation is nearer now than when we first believed. The night is nearly over; the day is almost here. So let us put aside the deeds of darkness and put on the armor of light. Let us behave decently, as in the daytime, not in carousing and drunkenness, not in sexual immorality and debauchery, not in dissension and jealousy. Rather, clothe yourselves with the Lord Jesus Christ, and do not think about how to gratify the desires of the flesh. (Romans 13:8-14)

In a women's Bible study with which I am involved, a friend shared her frustration with a coworker who is turned off by the ungodly attitude and actions of many of the outspoken Christians in her workplace. Consequently, she doesn't want to have anything to do with the God they claim to follow. It breaks my heart to hear stories like this, but unfortunately, it reveals a cold, hard truth. Christians sometimes turn people away from Christ by their unloving, hypocritical actions. Focusing on trying to do right naturally leads to a judgmental spirit such as this. If we think we can "be a better Christian" in our own strength, then our pride puffs us up and we give ourselves permission to measure everyone else according to our own standards. Then, we come across as being cold, unloving and harsh.

Author and minister William Barclay also noticed this pattern. He said, "More people have been brought into the church by the kindness of real Christian love than by all the theological arguments in the world, and more people have been driven from the church by the hardness and ugliness of so-called Christianity than by all the doubts in the world." So how do we draw people and not drive them away?

Love is the fulfillment of the law. Love is impossible in our inherently selfish spirits, but this passage gives two steps to take toward love; getting away from fleshly temptations, and getting into Christ's Spirit. Only through Christ can we put on the armor of light, giving God the freedom to love through us and keep us within His commandments. Only by giving up our own desires and surrendering to the Spirit are we able to overlook others' issues and love them right where they are. . . in much the same way Jesus does for us. In this way, people are drawn to God's love in us instead of being repulsed by our ugly, sinful nature. So, how do we love one another? We can't. Only God is able, so we must let Him love through us.

> *People need love, especially*
> *when they don't deserve it.*

How do you tend to judge others based on your own standards?

Do you find yourself trying to be a "good Christian" instead of letting God transform you into the image of Christ?

Heavenly Father,
It is easy for me to get caught up in trying to become the woman You created me to be. After much trial and error, I find this pursuit impossible. Instead of putting forth my best effort to bring about a transformation, it is my desire that I instead submit my whole life into Your hands, so You can mold me as You see fit.
In Jesus' Name I pray,
Amen

Fifty Two Days of Grace

A Heart of Acceptance

"Accept the one whose faith is weak, without quarreling over disputable matters. One person's faith allows them to eat anything, but another, whose faith is weak, eats only vegetables. The one who eats everything must not treat with contempt the one who does not, and the one who does not eat everything must not judge the one who does, for God has accepted them. Who are you to judge someone else's servant? To their own master, servants stand or fall. And they will stand, for the Lord is able to make them stand." (Romans 14:1-4)

Judging. We Christians love to judge each other. It seems to come so naturally and we justify our actions by claiming we are helping to keep our brother or sister on track. Truthfully, however, we are judging them in our hearts.

There are some things we must agree on. Jesus is God. Jesus came to earth in human form. Jesus died on the cross. Jesus rose from the dead. These are the foundations of our faith and are therefore considered to be indisputable. Then, there are the disputable matters. How and when we worship. The style of music used in church. How we should dress. What music we should listen to and movies we should watch. These kinds of choices should be made as a result of consulting with our Father. What may be acceptable for one believer could be a huge source of temptation for another. In these issues, each one of us will come to a different conclusion. And here is where the judging begins.

In my heart, I know that God does not want me to browse the Sunday newspaper advertisements because it undermines my spirit of contentment and breeds a desire to buy stuff I really don't need. So, I stay away from that temptation. If I have a friend over and she pours over the ads, discussing the pros and cons of all the latest home products, I become uncomfortable and begin to wonder in my heart if she is really as strong of a Christian as I thought she was. She appears to be so materialistic! But God is working on different issues in her life, and I have to respect her relationship with God, not assuming that she is being disobedient by doing the very thing I can't do.

We each are accountable to our Master. He alone knows our heart and what He has called us to do. Standing together as believers means we respect that relationship and don't assume to know what is best for each person. "There is only one Lawgiver and Judge, the one who is able to save and destroy. But you—who are you to judge your neighbor?" (James 4:12) God gives us enough to work on in our own lives without taking on everyone else's issues as well.

Fifty Two Days of Grace

Keep your eyes on Jesus,
not your neighbor.

Do you find it easier to judge another's sin than your own?

When do you assume your brother or sister is straying because they are partaking in an activity that is not good for you?

Heavenly Father,
I admit that I am quick to judge another while I give myself a pass. Help me to keep my eyes on Jesus, focusing on the path on which He is leading me. I know it is Your desire that I love others as You have loved me. I open my heart to let Your love flow through me.
In Jesus' Name I pray,
Amen

Fifty Two Days of Grace

Self-Fulfillment?

"One person considers one day more sacred than another; another considers every day alike. Each of them should be fully convinced in their own mind. Whoever regards one day as special does so to the Lord. Whoever eats meat does so to the Lord, for they give thanks to God; and whoever abstains does so to the Lord and gives thanks to God. For none of us lives for ourselves alone, and none of us dies for ourselves alone. If we live, we live for the Lord; and if we die, we die for the Lord. So, whether we live or die, we belong to the Lord. For this very reason, Christ died and returned to life so that he might be the Lord of both the dead and the living.

"You, then, why do you judge your brother or sister? Or why do you treat them with contempt? For we will all stand before God's judgment seat. It is written:

'As surely as I live,' says the Lord, 'every knee will bow before me; every tongue will acknowledge God.'

So then, each of us will give an account of ourselves to God." (Romans 14:5-12)

"My life is not my own." I can't count the number of times I disgustingly uttered this phrase under my breath as a mother of triplet daughters and their older sister. Raising four girls who are within two years of each other was never dull. In fact, during the early years I had few precious moments to myself, prompting me to utter the above phrase. As difficult yet rewarding as those years were, God was teaching me through it the truth that we find in today's passage. Our life does not belong to us to do with as we please. In fact, the moment we can let go of the notion of self-fulfillment, the more content and filled with peace we will become. When we live to fulfill God's plan for our life, we will feel satisfied and be less inclined to judge the choices others make. Each of us will stand before God's judgment seat and answer for our own life; it is not our place to assume to know the choices our brother or sister is making are wrong. We do not know God's plan for their lives, only God knows (Jeremiah 29:11).

Author and lecturer James Hitchcock hit the nail on the head concerning this issue. He said, "The search for self-fulfillment is endless, and endlessly frustrating." If the goal for our life is to never feel a sense of purpose, then we need look no further than our heart's desire. But, if our goal is to know that there is a reason for our being, we need to look to God and obediently do His bidding. "For we are God's workmanship, created in Christ Jesus to do good works, which God prepared in advance for us to do." (Ephesians 2:10)   What is stopping us from doing what God has planned for us? Fear? Greed? Selfishness? Comfort? Whatever it is, surrender it to Jesus and begin to live for Him. We will never feel more fulfilled as when we do what He has prepared for us to do!

Instead of shooting for self-fulfillment,
aim for God-fulfillment.

How are your life choices based on what will bring you the most contentment or pleasure?

Which areas of your life do you most struggle with submitting to God?

Heavenly Father,
I am often led by my fleshly desires. Therefore, it is my intention that I let go of my own will and let You have Your way in my life. I know that once I begin this process, I will experience much peace as I walk in tandem with your Spirit. I ask for the grace and mercy I need to let go of my own ways and let You rule in my heart.
In Jesus' Name I pray,
Amen

Fifty Two Days of Grace

Acceptance

"We who are strong ought to bear with the failings of the weak and not to please ourselves. Each of us should please our neighbors for their good, to build them up. For even Christ did not please himself but, as it is written: 'The insults of those who insult you have fallen on me.' For everything that was written in the past was written to teach us, so that through the endurance taught in the Scriptures and the encouragement they provide we might have hope.

"May the God who gives endurance and encouragement give you the same attitude of mind toward each other that Christ Jesus had, so that with one mind and one voice you may glorify the God and Father of our Lord Jesus Christ.

"Accept one another, then, just as Christ accepted you, in order to bring praise to God." (Romans 15:1-7)

We are a difficult bunch, we Christians. We have the reputation of being hard on others, and expecting more out of each other than we do out of ourselves. We are known for ripping brothers and sisters apart when they don't live up to the standards we have set. But this passage speaks of another reputation. Our reputation is to be that of a group of people who accepts one another right where we are, just as Christ accepts us (v 7). He doesn't wait for us to have our act together before we can come to Him. He asks us to come to Him as we are. In that state, we are a motley crew! We have problems coming out of our ears resulting in messy lives, but Jesus accepts us and enters into a relationship with us despite the chaos. Then, as His body, we come together and drive each other crazy.

There is something about our sin nature that is intolerant. I'm sure it has to do with our pride. Thomas á Kempis, a medieval monk, puts it in a nutshell when he said, "Be not angry that you cannot make others as you wish them to be, since you cannot make yourself as you wish to be." Ouch. If we cannot even clean up the mess in our own lives, what makes us think we can do so in others? God is in charge of cleaning up messes, and only He knows when and how best to accomplish this task. It is our job to accept one another through the process and give God the control He needs to do His job. In criticizing others, it is as if we are telling God, "Your way is just not working. Let me have a crack at it."

*Acceptance is hard, but yielding to God's
grace will bring praise to Him*

How do you spend more time on other's problems than on your own?

When do you find it difficult to look past the imperfections of a brother or sister?

Fifty Two Days of Grace

Heavenly Father,

Thank You for meeting me right where I am, in the middle of my sinful state. As a sinner saved by grace, it is easy for me to forget how helpless I am to save myself. Help me to always keep my true identity at the forefront of my mind so that I can extend the grace to others You so freely bestow upon me.

In Jesus' Name I pray,

Amen

Fifty Two Days of Grace

Lean on Me

"We who are strong ought to bear with the failings of the weak and not to please ourselves. Each of us should please our neighbors for their good, to build them up. For even Christ did not please himself but, as it is written: 'The insults of those who insult you have fallen on me.' For everything that was written in the past was written to teach us, so that through the endurance taught in the Scriptures and the encouragement they provide we might have hope.

"May the God who gives endurance and encouragement give you the same attitude of mind toward each other that Christ Jesus had, so that with one mind and one voice you may glorify the God and Father of our Lord Jesus Christ.

"Accept one another, then, just as Christ accepted you, in order to bring praise to God." (Romans 15:1-7)

I have a friend who is about to lose her job and also has several health conditions that make everyday activity nearly unbearable. She lives in constant pain. As she was sharing some of her struggles, she told me she didn't want to burden anyone with her problems. I have to admit, my first reaction was to feel irritated that she would want to bear that load herself when God clearly designed us to live together, rejoicing and grieving together. But to bear with one another means to be patient with each other's weaknesses, not just supporting each other in our trials and tribulations.

Jesus showed us what this looked like when He bore our sins on the cross. He did not chastise us, condemn us, lecture us, try to change us or say, "You should know better!" Instead, He bore our sins out of love. What would that look like if we had the same attitude? No gossip disguised as prayer requests, no analyzing others' situations and giving advice, but carrying each other's burdens and accepting one another just as Christ accepts each of us (v 5-7).

It might look like some trees that weathered a rare snow storm in North Carolina. As they held the 6 inches of heavy, wet snow, the smaller, weaker trees were able to lean on the stronger more mature trees for support. The branches from the trees which stood alone, however, snapped under the pressure of the load. We are designed to support each other, but we must be willing to lend that support without judgment, accepting one another's weaknesses just as the silent trees bore the weight of the weaker trees' burdens. God is praised when His creation behaves in the way He designed it to behave.

Acceptance is how we bear one another's failings. Judgment is reserved for God.

When do you struggle to accept a friend just the way she is?

How would your support demonstrate the love that God has poured out to you?

Heavenly Father,

I praise You for the way You have created me to live in community with the family of God. Help me to accept those around me in the same way that You accept me. Please give me the grace I need to be able to love them as You love me.
In Jesus' Name I pray,
Amen

Fifty Two Days of Grace

The Great Unifier

"For I tell you that Christ has become a servant of the Jews on behalf of God's truth, so that the promises made to the patriarchs might be confirmed and, moreover, that the Gentiles might glorify God for his mercy. As it is written: 'Therefore I will praise you among the Gentiles; I will sing the praises of your name.'"
(Romans 15:8-9)

"[The Lord] said to Abraham, 'Through your offspring all peoples on earth would be blessed.'" (Acts 3:25) If you are not a Jew, but know Jesus as your Savior, you have the God of all mercies to thank. Through Jesus Christ, God's many promises are fulfilled, including the one written above. The God of Abraham, Isaac and Jacob is now the God of all people!

Think of all the people groups existing in the world today; we are as diverse as the colors on the color wheel, yet all can call on the One and Only God as our very own. He is the great Unifier.

President Obama won the Nobel Peace Prize for his unifying spirit and message of hope. With all the talk of peace and efforts to bring people together, however, Jesus is the only One qualified to do it. He is the One able to tear down barriers of culture and tradition and give us all a spirit of unity. The UN can't do it. Barak Obama can't do it. Martin Luther King Jr. couldn't do it. As wonderful as their messages of hope and acceptance are and were, they pale in comparison to what Jesus did by sacrificing His life. In that act of mercy, He opened the doors of true hope. Hope in an eternal peace that can dwell in our hearts and that defies understanding. Hope in a unity of people everywhere who trust in Christ as their Savior. This is the only peace we will ever witness this side of heaven!

Thank God for His message of peace found through the great Unifier: Jesus Christ our Lord.

When do you turn to other sources to find peace?

Are you easily caught up in popular political or social movements that offer benefits that are only found in Christ?

Heavenly Father,

I admit that I spend a lot of time searching for meaning in life. I have a great desire for peace, but often overlook the Truth I read in Your Word. I praise You for being a God who draws people unto Himself and can create a family out of a myriad of tribes and nations. Jesus Christ is truly the great Unifier. Help me to always place all my hope in Him.

In Jesus' Name I pray,

Amen

About the Author

Cindy is a sinner saved by grace whose faith in God's willingness to use even the most broken among us has given her a passion for encouraging others to live the abundant life that is offered through Jesus Christ. She is devoted to her husband of 25 years, and is most proud of their four daughters who continue to astound her with their faith.

Read more of her work at:
http://cindyspostscripts.blogspot.com/

Made in the USA
Lexington, KY
21 November 2019

57443676R00107